This book is a
Special Gift

from

---

to

---

on the occasion of

---

date

SEEDS OF DESTINY Classics

VOLUME 1

PAUL ENENCHE MD

SEEDS OF DESTINY CLASSICS

Published by
Destiny Publications,
Beside Old Federal Secretariat,
Area I, Garki, Abuja, Nigeria. P.M.B 1677
Tel: 08072323270 and 08033144509

Unless otherwise indicated, all scriptures are taken from
King James Version of the Bible.

Designed & Printed by
asbotgraphics LIMITED

Dr. Paul & Dr. (Mrs.) Becky
Enenche

INTRODUCTION

The word of God is the container of the mind and thought of God. It is inspired by His spirit, given to His prophets and written by the guided hands of His anointed scribes. It is a collection of timeless instructions, admonitions, revelations, insights, inspirations and prophecies.

The word of God is calculated for the profits of His people. It is the word that reveals to the child of God, both his origin and his creator. This revelation enhances his relationship and fellowship with God. And when this relationship is established, the word enhances the believer's awareness of his rights and privileges in God. It guarantees their safety and preservation in a world infested with evil and satanic operations. The word of God is also a package of supernatural favour and blessing for the people of God. The word is an inseparable companion and guide of the believer on his pilgrimage on earth.

But how does one maximise all the benefits of the word of God as mentioned above. It is by doing the following:

1. **INTEREST**: Interest brings insight. God will not give insight where there is no interest Hosea 6:1-3

2. **VALUE**: Value brings insight. God does not give the precious to the one who does not value it (Matt. 7:6). The word of God is a precious treasure.

3. **HUNGER**: Hunger brings insight. Spiritual hunger is key to accessing spiritual treasures (insights).

4. **FOCUS:** Light travels in the direction of focus (Matt. 6:22-23). Focus achieved via quietness and separation gives access to wisdom.

5. **FERVENCY:** Being fervent in the Spirit with spiritual intensity births insight (1 Cor. 2:9-10)

6. **EXCITEMENT:** Excitement brings insight. The treasures of salvation and the word are drawn with the agency of joy (Isaiah 12:3).

The Seed of Destiny Classic Series is designed to enhance both deep interest and readability because of its topical arrangement. This will make for your high sense of value for the word of God which will in turn increase your hunger and focus. This focus and consistent reading of the processed word of God will enhance your spiritual fervency and vibrancy thereby making you more excited and joyful as you come to the knowledge of your liberty and other benefits of redemption.

The material in your hand (the Seeds of Destiny Classic Series) is a compilation of the processed word of God collected from some of the previous editions of the daily Devotional, Seeds of Destiny right from its inception. It is a wealth of inspiration and powerful insights from the word of God that will spur you into greater feats and fulfilment in life. I pray that you will find it a worthy companion in your walk with God and pilgrimage on earth.

Dr. Paul Enenche.

1

What To Do When You Don't Know What To Do.

O our God, wilt thou not judge them? for we have no might against this great company that cometh against us; neither know we what to do: but our eyes are upon thee. **– 2 CHRON 20:12**

JEHOSHAPHAT and the children of Israel were greatly threatened and overwhelmed by the children of Moab, Amon and Edom (Mount Seir) in battle. It was a situation beyond their physical strength and strategy; they didn't know what to do. The question is, what do you do in a situation like this?

The first thing is to slow down on activity, admit your ignorance of what to do and be still (calm) knowing that there will always be a way out.

When the children of Israel were confronted with the Red sea while at the same time being pursued by the

Egyptians, the Lord told them to stand still and see His salvation. The point is, never struggle to get something done by all means or continue business as usual when you don't know what to do. It is as disastrous as a blind man running wildly or a man trying to repair a car he knows nothing about.

KEY THOUGHT

Those who look up to God will never look down in shame.

The next thing is to look up to the Lord for instruction, direction, inspiration and revelation because He knows what to do (2 Chron. 20:12). Those who look up to God can never be let down by Him. If you are at the mercy of God, you are no longer at the mercy of the devil!

Remember this: ***Those who look up to God will never look down in shame.***

COUNSEL

1. Draw action points from the recommended message.
2. Compare your steps with the lessons learnt, and then move into action.

For further understanding, get this message: *What To Do When You Don't Know What To Do.*

BOOK QUOTE: ***Those who apply mentality cannot be victims of satanic captivity.*** Culled from *10 PRINCIPAL SECRETS OF PRINCIPAL PEOPLE* by Dr Paul Enenche.

(From Wednesday, 28th November 2012)

2

Help Through Impartation

I am the vine, ye are the branches: He that abideth in me, and I in him, the same bringeth forth much fruit: for without me ye can do nothing. – JOHN 15:5

THE powerfulness of God is revealed when the helplessness of man is recognised. The help of God makes you the choice of God. And when you become the choice of God, you become a voice to your generation. So to end as a voice, you must start with His help. And you can either receive it directly from God or He may choose to use someone whom He has helped to help you. This is so because there are people who have as a manifestation, what is still to you a revelation. They have an increased measure of anointing, insight, or wisdom in the area you desire to excel.

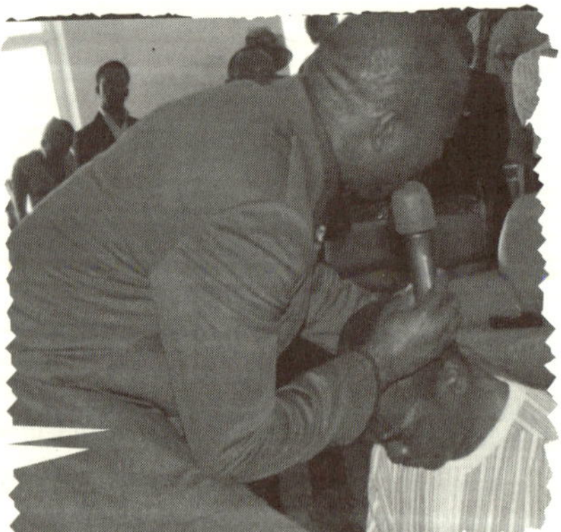

> **KEY THOUGHT**
> ***The powerfulness of God is revealed when the helplessness of man is recognised.***

The truth is, we all have equality of destiny by redemption but we have differences in grace by impartation. When therefore you encounter a higher level of grace or recognise it in anyone, wisdom demands that you humble yourself before such a grace for your own good.

As we said earlier, the help of God is the answer to the weakness of man. The help of God also makes a life that is oppressed to be set free. When you are helped of God, the Almighty God undertakes to fight for you and frustrates whoever or whatever tries to oppress you. It is unsafe therefore to resist or oppress a man who is enjoying the help of God because God who is also his defence sponsors his strength. It is wisdom therefore to make demands on the help of God in times of challenge.

Remember this: ***the powerfulness of God is revealed when the helplessness of man is recognised.***

COUNSEL

1. Identify godly men who have the help of God clearly on their lives.
2. Find out how they secured the help of God.
3. Pray passionately for them and follow their steps

For further understanding, get this message: Impartation Of Grace.

BOOK QUOTE: ***Every relationship that you must profit from must cost you something.*** Culled from *365 WISDOM CAPSULES* by Dr Paul Enenche.

(From Monday, 7th November 2011)

3

Faith Sets The Limit For Your Provision.

But without faith it is impossible to please him: for he that cometh to God must believe that he is, and that he is a rewarder of them that diligently seek him. **– HEB. 11:6**

WHAT HAS NOT been achieved is not what is impossible; it is what has not been attempted. And faith is the foundation for all possibilities. The Bible says in Mark 9:23 ... '*If thou canst believe, all things are possible to him that believeth.*' The meaning is, your possibilities are determined by your 'believe-ability'.

Nothing is impossible if unbelief is not available. The limit of your conviction is the limit of your provision. Where your faith stops is where your provision stops. Your possibilities can only go as far as your faith goes. Manifestations only run out when you run out of faith.

Manifestations cannot be in short supply when faith is not in short supply.

> **KEY THOUGHT**
>
> ***Your possibilities are determined by your 'believe-ability'.***

Faith is the supernatural currency by which supernatural transactions are made. If you want an exchange in the supernatural, only faith can guarantee it. Faith has the capacity to blast-off impossibilities into obscurity. Build your faith today by the Word of God and pray in the spirit.

Remember this: ***your possibilities are determined by your believe-ability.***

COUNSEL

1. Increase your Word intake, read books, and listen to messages on faith.
2. Pray more in the spirit in order to build your faith. (Jude Vs 20)

For further understanding, get this message: Mental Renovation.

BOOK QUOTE ***In the walk of faith, you start even when you can't see the end.*** Culled from *365 WISDOM CAPSULES* by Dr Paul Enenche.

(From Saturday, 12th November 2011)

4

What You See Is What You Can Seize.

And the Lord said unto Abram, after that Lot was separated from him, Lift up now thine eyes, and look from the place where thou art northward, and southward, and eastward, and westward: For all the land which thou seest, to thee will I give it… **GEN 13:14-15**

THE problem many people have with fulfilling destiny is that they have fixed their eyes on where we are, instead of where we can be. But God's plan is that we look at where we are going and look away from where they are.

You see, you can't move from where you are until you look away from where you are. Those who go far see far. Where you are going should become the major preoccupation of your mind. If you are not married yet, begin to see your husband or wife. If you are not currently employed, begin to see yourself working. When you look at where you are, all that happens is that

you become frustrated and depressed in life. That is why you must look away from where you are.

KEY THOUGHT

You can't move from where you are until you look away from where you are.

In Micah 2:10, the Bible says, '*Arise ye, and depart; for this is not your rest: because it is polluted, it shall destroy you, even with a sore destruction.*' Look away from that predicament now: that unemployment, barrenness, singleness, lack, etc., and realise that they are not your resting place. If you focus on them, you will be frustrated and destroyed. Arise and depart from them! Look away from them! Look at the future.

Remember this: ***you can't move from where you are until you look away from where you are.***

COUNSEL

1. Put God's vision for your life in front of you.
2. See yourself there

For further understanding, get this message: Vision And Favour.

BOOK QUOTE ***A change of vision produces a change of level. A change of level also produces a change of vision.*** Culled from *365 WISDOM CAPSULES* by Dr Paul Enenche.

(from Sunday, 28th August 2011)

5

Mentality for Relevance.

***And in all matters of wisdom and understanding, that the king inquired of them, he found them ten times better than all the magicians and astrologers that were in all his realm.* – DAN. 1:20**

TO be relevant in your generation, you need high-level mental soundness and agility. You were created in the image of God and so, everywhere you find yourself, you must realise that you are meant to reason like someone created in the image of God. It is an abomination therefore to receive a query at your place of work for poor performance. The wisdom of God is designed to make you to be preferred above others at your place of work. Daniel was preferred above all other wise men in Babylon because of the wisdom of God at work in his life. He was relevant throughout the reign of four kings.

Actually, anytime a Christian who has the mind of God is transferred from an office, the organization, and especially

the boss should regret the posting. It should be difficult for people to discard you as irrelevant. Truth is, if your presence is not felt, your absence will not be noticed. And you can make your presence felt by proving your relevance which can be achieved by mental exercise.

KEY THOUGHT

Never feel like you have arrived; learn new things daily.

Mental exercise is the key to a life of excellence. Never feel that you know too much. Never feel that you have arrived. Exercise your mind, learn new things daily, do new things, improve yourself and your relevance cannot be denied.

Mentality affects relevance. Work on your mentality today and your relevance tomorrow is guaranteed.

Remember this: ***never feel like you have arrived; learn new things daily.***

COUNSEL

1. Do a character study of the life of Daniel to discover the secret of his high mentality and excellence.
2. Apply Daniel's principle to your life and current assignment.

For further understanding, get this message: Mentality For Prosperity.

BOOK QUOTE ***Those who apply mentality cannot be victims of satanic captivity.*** Culled from *WISDOM WAYS* by Dr Paul Enenche.

(From Sunday, 5th June 2011)

6

Develop A Warfare Mentality.

***And David said unto Saul, Thy servant kept his father's sheep, and there came a lion, and a bear, and took a lamb out of the flock: And I went out after him, and smote him...* – 1 SAM 17:34-35**

TO succeed in life, you need a sense of responsibility – a sense of duty to your assignment. You also need a sense of purpose, knowing that you must not leave this world as a failure. You must determine that whatever it takes positively to succeed, you will give it.

You must understand that it takes a warring spirit to succeed in life. No one will fight your battles for you; you must war with the devil to secure your destiny. If a strange woman is after your husband, for instance, you must fight the battle on your knees and take back your husband. It is a better way to fight than confront her physically.

It takes discovery to attain recovery. Discover the purpose for which you are alive; discover your strength and you will recover that which the enemy has stolen from you. Davi discovered his strength (lion and bear killing) and that helped him put away the shame before Israel, by killing goliath.

KEY THOUGHT

It takes discovery to attain recovery.

Every human being has certain strength. Discovering yours will strengthen you to war against the devil more efficiently and effectively.

Remember this: ***it takes discovery to attain recovery.***

COUNSEL

1. Always remember that the devil is a defeated foe waiting to be bound in hell.
2. Before confronting the devil, know your victory promises in God from the Scriptures. Also know your strength in God

For further understanding, get this message: Dedication despite distraction.

BOOK QUOTE ***Do not get to a point where there is a problem that makes you turn your back.*** Culled from *WISDOM WAYS* by Dr Paul Enenche.

(From Tuesday, 21st June 2011)

7 Two Kinds Of People.

Jesus said unto him, If thou canst believe, all things are possible to him that believeth. **– Mark 9:23**

YOUR MOUNTAIN is the springboard from where God expects you to take your flight to greatness. All things are possible to him who believes. You can move from where you are now to where God wants you to be. Possibilities are at the disposal of the believer.

There are two classes of people on earth: pessimists and optimists. Pessimists are people who see only negativity and impossibilities in every situation; optimists are those who see positivity and possibilities in similar situations. Pessimists never take a decision in the direction of possibilities because they cannot see it, therefore, cannot decide for it.

In fact, your outcome in life is determined by your mentality. The way you see things determines the way things happen in your life. What you see coming your way eventually comes; what you don't see never comes.

Inside every adversity, there is advancement. Your ability to see advancement releases the possibility of its manifestation. What determines your destiny is the path you choose to tread the path of possibility or negativity, optimism or pessimism. One key to the fulfilment of destiny is the ability to see possibility in the midst of impossibility – the ability to be optimistic when the circumstances of life try to impose pessimism on you.

KEY THOUGHT

The way you see things determines the way things happen in your life.

Change your mentality and your destiny will change.

Remember this: ***the way you see things determines the way things happen in your life.***

COUNSEL

1. Beware of the people you relate with and the materials you consume such as books, messages, movies, etc.
2. Associate with optimistic-minded people and mentors.
3. Always look out for the possibility in every seeming adversity

For further understanding, get this message: Winning the fight of faith.

BOOK QUOTE ***The voice of the person you listen to determines where you will end in life.*** Culled from *WISDOM WAYS* by Dr Paul Enenche.

(From Sunday 28th August, 2011)

8

Live And Fight For A Cause.

***And David said, What have I now done? Is there not a cause?* – 1 Sam 17:29**

NOTHING is impossible! All that is required is a little time to prove its possibility. In 1904, when the Wright brothers made their move to invent the airplane, people asked them whether they had ever seen iron fly in the air. They were questioned on the grounds of gravity but that didn't change their minds. Today, it is possible to travel from one continent to another in a matter of hours by air instead of months by sea. This is possible because some persons believed it was possible when everyone else said it was not.

If your possibilities must be realised, then you must not give up when others do. To do this, however, you must be a man or a woman of purpose. Consider the story of David as he made his intention to fight Goliath known. His brothers attacked him verbally with the aim of discouraging him

from such a venture. Hear what he said, 'What *have I now done? Is there not a cause?*' (1 Sam 17:29). David had a cause (purpose). He wanted his brothers to know that he had taken personal responsibility for the success of the battle in order to end the blasphemy and curses from Goliath. He accepted the responsibility to be the extension of God's Hand that would slay Goliath and end the shame in Israel.

KEY THOUGHT

Never feel like you have arrived; learn new things daily.

When responsibility is clear and accepted, possibility is easy. When you know your responsibility, you are exposed to your possibilities.

Remember this: ***if your possibility must be realised, then you must not give up when others do.***

COUNSEL:

1. Ensure that the cause you live your life for is both clear and in line with God's vision.
2. Refuse to live for a cause that pleases only self.

For further understanding, get this message: Winning the fight of faith.

BOOK QUOTE ***When you come to that point where you cannot be confused about what you want and you cannot be convinced against it, then no devil or man can stand between you and what you desire.*** Culled from *10 PRINCIPAL SECRETS OF PRINCIPAL PEOPLE* by Dr Paul Enenche.

(From Sunday, 5th June 2011)

9

A Disciple Ought To Be Disciplined.

No man that warreth entangleth himself with the affairs of this life; that he may please him who hath chosen him to be a soldier. – 2 Tim. 2:4

THE CHRISTIAN race and Church work can be likened to the military setting, which is highly regimented. When God is preparing a man, He does a thorough job on him.

Part of that thorough job includes the impartation focus, self-denial, and strict discipline. The training process may not be easy but you are admonished to endure hardness like a good soldier (2 Tim. 2:3).

A soldier is taught punctuality and respect for order and authority. Christians should learn to be punctual, especially Church workers, because every Church service is an appointment with God. No soldier keeps his superior officer waiting, therefore, you shouldn't keep God waiting.

KEY THOUGHT
Every Church service is an appointment with God... don't keep Him waiting.

It is a pity that some Christians treat their leaders and pastors with contempt. Soldiers are respectful.

Some believers do in the Church what they would never do in their offices. While they have regards for their bosses and observe office regulations, they treat Church rules and regulations with disdain. It is certainly sad that men fear fellow men whom they see and disrespect the authority set up by God in Church, possibly because they do not see God physically. Embrace discipline today and you would be glad you did.

Remember this: ***every Church service is an appointment with God....don't keep Him waiting.***

COUNSEL:

1. Submit to the authority of God through the Church.
2. Never be among those who treat the things of God with levity such as littering the house of God with dirt.

For further understanding, get this message: The Place Of Mentoring In Ministry.

BOOK QUOTE: *Charisma can take you to the top but it is character that can keep or sustain you there.* Culled from *10 SUCCESS STRATEGIES FOR RELATIONSHIP* by Dr (Mrs) Becky Enenche.

(From Sunday, 27th March 2011)

10

God's Agenda.

***But as truly as I live, all the earth shall be filled with the glory of the LORD* – NUMBER 14:21**

OUR PASSAGE today reveals God's mission statement. His agenda is to fill the earth with His Presence, Power, Principles, and Glory. He intends to establish His rule and reign on earth. He intends to multiply His Own quality of people on the face of the earth. In the words of evangelist Reinhard Bonnke, 'He plans to plunder hell and populate Heaven.' He wants to dethrone the enemy and enthrone the Almighty on earth.

What is your role in this plan?

1. Share your personal experience of the Lord with the people around you. Let them know the changes taking place in your life since you came to the knowledge

of the Lord. Let them know the difference that knowing the Lord has made in your life since you knew Him.

2. Show your world the kindness, love and character of God. Demonstrate to your spouse, family, colleagues at work and neighbours the love-life and character of God that is available in your life. Someone once said, 'Unbelievers do not have the Bible and even if they do, they do not read them. Christians are the Bibles that unbelievers read.' Please ensure that they read the correct thing from your life.

KEY THOUGHT

Christians are the Bibles that unbelievers read.

Remember this: ***Christians are the Bibles that unbelievers read.***

COUNSEL:

1. Do as you have read. Be part of the fulfilling of God's agenda on earth.

For Further Understanding, Get This Message: The Power Of Love.

BOOK QUOTE: ***When you represent God well, He rewards you well***. Culled from *365 WISDOM CAPSULES* by Dr Paul Enenche.

(From Sunday, 3rd May 2009)

11

Be a Kingdom Advertising Agent.

How beautiful upon the mountains are the feet of him that bringeth good tidings, that publisheth peace; that bringeth good tidings of good, that publisheth salvation; that saith unto Zion, thy God reigneth – **ISAIAH 52:7**

THERE IS A REALM of beauty, blessedness, and elevation that is reserved for men and women who are advertising agents for the Kingdom of God. It is profitable to become one of them.

How do you become one?

1. Share your own testimonies and those of others with the people in your life like the woman of Samaria did (John 4:28-29). Let people know of both the goodness and awesomeness of God through your testimony. Afterwards, you can offer to bring them to Church to experience the same.

2. Become a distributor of gospel materials such as Bibles,

Devotional like Seeds of Destiny, tapes, CDs, VCDs, DVDs, etc., to loved ones and those you come into contact with. Literally, fill the world around you with His principles, Power, and glory contained in those materials.

KEY THOUGHT

To advertise for God is to advance in life.

3. Play the CDs, DVDs, etc. in your restaurant, barbing, or hair dressing salon, shop, the commercial transport you operate, your personal car, etc.

4. Make your home, office, shop, etc., available as a sanctuary of the Lord for Home Church, a place of succour, etc.

When you are able to do any of the above and more, you literally position yourself for the blessedness, beauty, and elevation that come from being a gospel-advertising agent.

Remember this: ***to advertise for God is to advance in life.***

COUNSEL:

1. Do as the passage says.
2. Be diligent in advertising the Kingdom of God.

For further understanding, get this message: Daniel's Secret of Authority.

BOOK QUOTE: ***It is better to be known for doing one thing well than be unknown because of doing everything wrong.*** Culled from *365 WISDOM CAPSULES* by Dr Paul Enenche.

(From Monday, 4th May 2009).

12

Five Things Not To Do Or Say

Whatever I have, wherever I am, I can make it through anything in the one who makes me who I am
– Phil. 4:13 (The Message Bible)

THERE ARE FIVE things you must never do or say and they are:

1. **Do not allow life to pass you by.** Do not allow yourself to be left behind. Be informed both spiritually and naturally. Make progress continuously, no matter how little.

2. **Do not live below your potential.** Do not live below your possibilities. Do not live below the life God planned for you to live. Expand your mind and life by the revelation of the Word and by continuous education.

> **KEY THOUGHT**
> ***The way you think affects the way you live and the results you see.***

3. Don't ever say, 'There is no time'. Know that time will never surrender itself to you because it is not what you wait for. Time is what you order, employ and direct.

4. Don't ever say 'I don't have the brain or ability'. There is nobody without the brain or ability to do what God wants them to do. The way you think affects the way you live and the results you see.

5. Don't ever say, 'I am too old or it is too late'. The fact is, it is never too late to start all over again if you didn't get it right the first time. May God give you the grace to move to that next level, in Jesus' Name.

Remember this: ***the way you think affects the way you live and the results you see.***

COUNSEL:

1. Go over what you have learnt above.
2. Change both your language and mentality.

For further understanding, get this message: Twenty-One Foolish Things People Do Parts 3&4

QUOTE: ***Words are seeds – life's harvests of today are the products of the Word seeds of yesterday.*** Culled from *22 LAWS OF LIFE* by Dr Paul Enenche.

(From Friday, 15th May 2009)

13

The Power Of Love

Howbeit as the disciples stood round about him, he rose up, and came into the city and the next day he departed with Barnabas to Derbe. **– ACTS 14:20**

BELOVED, love is the strongest power on earth. It is stronger than the power of death. It brought the apostle Paul back to life as our anchor text shows. What is the focus of love?

1. Love focuses on giving meaning, purpose and value to the lives of people that God brings our way, like our husband, wife, boss, client, etc. That is, when people come in contact with you, they will feel the love of God; their self-worth and value will be enhanced by the way you relate with them.

2. Love focuses also on giving others satisfaction by relieving their fears, worries and agitation. This is achieved by displaying genuine interest in the needs of other people.

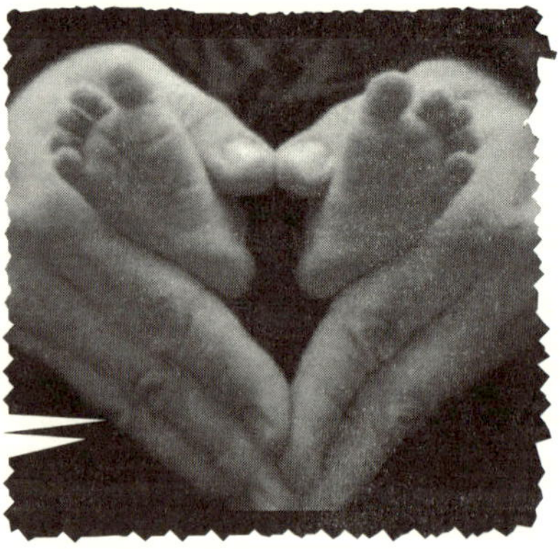

3. Love focuses on doing for others what we expect them to do for us, treating others the way we expect them to treat us. It is putting ourselves in the shoes of others and becoming sensitive to their pains (Matt. 7:12).

KEY THOUGHT

The strongest power on earth is the power of love.

4. Love focuses on generosity. Love makes you think of what to do or give to those in your life. Love makes you ask questions such as, 'In what way can I be a blessing to this or that person?'

5. Love focuses on an existence that is free of bitterness, malice or strife. Love makes you go out of your way to ensure that tension or strife is eliminated from your life.

Beloved, get connected to the power of love. It is the Power of God. It will change everything around you.

Remember this: ***the strongest power on earth is the power of love.***

COUNSEL

1. Love is a practice; therefore, commence the practice of love and begin to perfect yourself in the love life.

For further understanding, get this message: The Missing Link - 3

BOOK QUOTE ***The practice of love provokes the Presence of God.*** Culled from *365 WISDOM CAPSULES* by Dr Paul Enenche.

(From Thursday, 21st May 2009)

14

You Are A Creature Of Value

'So God created man in his own image, in the image of God created he him; male and female created he them'
– GEN. 1:27

THE QUALITY of every product is determined by the integrity and reputation of its manufacturer. For example, when a product is manufactured in some countries like the UK or Japan, you are sure of its quality and standard. If a product is made by the Almighty God, how much more valuable and qualitative then would it be in comparison to any earthly product. You are a product of quality and value because you were made by God.

The value and quality of a product can also be known by the cost of its production or the price of its purchase. It cost God the sacrifice of His Only Begotten Son to

purchase you (1 Cor. 6:20). You must therefore learn to love, value and appreciate your life. Your value in life is neither determined by the circumstances of your birth past failures, mistakes and errors, nor is it determined by human verdict or opinion. Your value in life is not determined by your height, complexion, sex or tribe. Your value in life is determined by the quality of your Maker as well as the cost of your purchase. God never made anybody to be of low or inferior quality.

> **KEY THOUGHT**
> ***You are a product of quality and value because you were made by God.***

You are a person of value! Do not undervalue yourself, and allow nobody to undervalue you.

Remember this: ***you are a product of quality and value because you are made by God.***

COUNSEL:

1. Appreciate God for making you a person of quality.
2. Begin to exist in the consciousness of your value

For further understanding, get this message: Himself Took Our Imfirmities.

BOOK QUOTE: ***Your content is what determines your worth. What you carry determines your value.*** Culled from *365 WISDOM CAPSULES* by Dr Paul Enenche.

(From Saturday, 23rd May 2009)

15

Functioning With the Anointing.

But my horn shalt thou exalt like the horn of a unicorn: I shall be anointed with fresh oil
— PSALM 92:10

EVERY CHILD OF GOD on earth needs the anointing of God to function successfully in life and ministry. The anointing of God is not just for full-time pastors or ministers. The anointing of God upon David caused him first to excel as a shepherd then later as a psalmist, songwriter, instrumentalist, expert warrior, inventor of musical instruments, leader (people developer), king, priest and prophet. The anointing of God upon Joseph (with which he dreamt and also interpreted dreams) eventually aided his appointment and success as a prime minister in Egypt.

The anointing of God upon Solomon also 'exploded' to a

point where he wrote 3,000 proverbs and 1,500 songs. He also excelled as an unusual businessman and speaker by that same anointing The anointing upon Daniel caused him to function as a prophet and excel as a government leader first in the Babylonian empire and later in the Medo-Persian Empire. Again, beloved, it is not just pastors that need the anointing on their lives. Such thinking is the reason for the limitation of most Christians. Abraham was not a pastor. He was a multi-millionaire livestock farmer who walked in the covenant and anointing of God. Upgrade your destiny and function with success and excellence in every realm of your life by operating under the anointing.

KEY THOUGHT

Every child of God on earth needs the anointing of God to function successfully in life and ministry.

Remember this: ***every child of God on earth needs the anointing of God to function successfully in life and ministry.***

COUNSEL

1. Be fully submissive to the spiritual authority placed over you.
2. Upgrade the quality of your time with God.

For further understanding, get this message: Anointing for all-round breakthrough.

BOOK QUOTE: ***Go for the Presence of God; it will open doors for you anywhere.*** Culled from *30 SECRETS TO THE TOP* by Dr Paul Enenche.

(From Sunday, 24th May 2009)

16

The Power of the Spirit.

***But if the Spirit of him that raised up Jesus from the dead dwell in you, he that raised up Christ from the dead shall also quicken your mortal bodies by his Spirit that dwelleth in you.* – ROM. 8:11**

THE POWER OF THE Holy Spirit was the Power that raised up Jesus Christ from the dead. Therefore, no one filled with the Holy Spirit is permitted to be held down. It is like a balloon filled with helium gas that must overcome gravity.

Beloved, the chief assignment of the Holy Ghost is to assist the sons of men to overcome limitation and establish their elevation. When the prophet Samuel anointed Saul, King of Israel, he was both uplifted and elevated. When David was anointed, he was also elevated and uplifted. The arrival of the Holy Ghost in the lives of the apostles marked the end of their seclusion, obscurity,

> **KEY THOUGHT**
>
> ***To be anointed is to be elevated and uplifted.***

and timidity. Beloved, you cannot carry the Power that created the world and remain tied down in misery. You cannot carry the Person and Power that created the world and your own life remains a wilderness. You cannot carry the Power that filled an empty earth with life in the beginning and your own life remains empty. You cannot carry the Presence and Power of the One that beautified the earth and your life remains ugly. You cannot carry the Power and Presence that lighted a dark earth in the beginning and your life remains buried in the darkness of confusion and evil works. Activate the Power of the Spirit in your life and begin to see unusual things.

Remember this: ***to be anointed is to be elevated and uplifted.***

COUNSEL

1. Re-read the message of today and begin to live in the consciousness of it.
2. If you are not yet baptised in the Holy Ghost, endeavour to get baptised and utilise the language of the Spirit in aggressive praying

For further understanding, get this message: The Spirit of Life.

BOOK QUOTE ***You may lose anything in life, but one thing you must never lose is the Presence of God.*** Culled from *30 SECRETS TO THE TOP* by Dr Paul Enenche.

(From Monday, 25th May 2009)

17 Are You Worth Fighting Against?

And when they were departed, behold, the angel of the Lord appeareth to Joseph in a dream, saying, Arise, and take the young child and his mother, and flee into Egypt, and be thou there until I bring thee word: for Herod will seek the young child to destroy him. – Matt 2:13

THE ENEMY FIGHTS greatness from infancy. I congratulate you if your life is characterised by battles from childhood. It is a sign of greatness. Satan fought Moses, David, Joseph, and our Lord Jesus Christ from infancy. When Jesus was born, Herod sought to kill Him. Satan also fought Esther from infancy; as a little girl, she lost her parents. Shadrach, Meshach and Abednego were not exempted. That is the point. Whenever the devil notices greatness and a bright future, he launches an attack.

My mother almost miscarried me at six weeks of pregnancy but the plans of the devil failed. Then when she went to the hospital to give birth after nine (9) months of pregnancy and in labour, they told her that she could not give birth there because according to them, she was not yet in labour. She replied, 'Don't I know labour again? This is my fifth pregnancy and you are telling me that I'm not in labour?' She was told to go back home. She came back home and gave birth to me and nobody was there. She cut the umbilical cord by herself and arranged the baby before anyone could know what was happening. This was the strategy of the enemy to kill the child (myself) before birth. Moreover, as the child was growing up, he was afflicted

> **KEY THOUGHT**
>
> ***Greatness in God is characterised by persistent fight from the enemy especially from infancy.***

with febrile convulsion. I could have ended up as an epileptic child because of repeated convulsions, but it is only God that has the final say. Greatness in God is usually characterised by persistent fight from the enemy especially from infancy

The reason is, the devil fights whom he fears. He fights anything and anyone he fears. If you are not worth fighting, you are not worth fearing. And if the devil is fighting you, congratulations! He fears you. And what the devil fears must come upon him. Again the devil is afraid of your destiny and that is why he fights you; and that destiny must come to pass, in Jesus' Name.

Remember this: ***greatness in God is characterised by persistent fight from the enemy especially from infancy.***

COUNSEL:

1. Live daily with a warfare mentality.
2. Identify the challenging issues of your life.
3. War it out with the devil.

For further understanding, get this message: The Power to Take it by Force.

BOOK QUOTE: ***There is no flight without a fight.*** Culled from *30 SECRETS TO THE TOP* by Dr. Paul Enenche.

(From Tuesday, July 9, 2013)

18

The Miracle Meal

***And Melchizedek king of Salem brought forth bread and wine: and he was the priest of the most high God. And he blessed him, and said, Blessed be Abram of the most high God, possessor of heaven and earth:* – GEN 14:18-19**

FROM OUR TEXT, Abraham received the blessing from Melchizedek when he gave him bread and wine. The blessing was released upon Abraham meaning that the curse was destroyed at that place of the communion. The communion releases God's blessing upon a man and destroys curses.

In 1 Samuel 21:6, Ahimelech gave David hallowed bread when he was running away from King Saul. That hallowed bread was his bread of escape. From that day forward, Saul could never catch him anymore and he escaped Saul's sword forever. The communion is a bread of escape. The demon (or death) that is looking for you cannot catch you if you connect to the mystery of the communion.

In John 6:53, Jesus said, '*Then Jesus said unto them, Verily, verily, I say unto you, Except ye eat the flesh of the Son of man, and drink his blood, ye have no life in you.*'

What then is the communion? It is the life of Jesus. Anything that Jesus carries is transferrable by the communion. The communion is the very life of Jesus. As you take it in, you take in God's life and the devil is rendered helpless about your life.

In what condition should you take the communion? 1 Corinthians 11:26-30 reveals that if a man takes the communion unworthily or in sin, he invites damnation, weakness and death into his life.

> **KEY THOUGHT**
>
> ***To be engaged in smoking, drinking, fornicating and still be taking the communion causes destruction instead of distinction.***

The communion is disastrous to a sinner. To be engaged in smoking, drinking, fornicating and still be taking the communion causes destruction instead of distinction. Taking the communion and living in sin is taking God for granted. This can cause some people to die because they take God for granted. The communion is powerful and transmits the very life of Jesus into your body. And whenever the communion is to be taken, it must not be taken religiously. You must understand that the communion is God's Life stepping into your body!

Remember this: ***to be engaged in smoking, drinking, fornicating and still be taking the communion causes destruction instead of distinction.***

ASSIGNMENTS

1. Take the communion as often as you can. Endeavour not to miss Communion services.
2. Endeavour to take the communion with the right mindset

FOR FURTHER UNDERSTANDING, GET THIS MESSAGE: The Communion of escape.

BOOK QUOTE: ***Mentality guarantees longevity. Mentality averts calamity. Mentality is the key to security.*** Culled from *15 KINGDOM STRATEGIES FOR SURVIVAL* by Dr Paul Enenche.

(from Wednesday, July 10, 2013)

19

Your Result Is Superior To Your Reproach

Fear not; for thou shalt not be ashamed: neither be thou confounded; for thou shalt not be put to shame: for thou shalt forget the shame of thy youth, and shalt not remember the reproach of thy widowhood any more.
– Isa 54:4

IN THE BIBLE, we are told of the city of Jabez. In 1st Chronicles 2:55, Jabez had a city and people dwelt in that city. In chapter 4 of the same 1 Chronicles, the Bible tells us about the frustration Jabez experienced. His impact was mentioned before his setback. What does this mean? It means that your result will be placed above your reproach. At the end of your journey in life, what will count is not what you suffered but what you offered; not what you passed through but what passed through you.

You are rated by your results, not your insult. Don't die with any reproach. And don't come to a point where you think that what has happened to you is a 'fixed deposit.' A time will come when people will not even remember what you used to pass through because of your overwhelming results. When you lie down at night, let the thoughts that fill your mind be centred on what God says about you, where you are going, where you desire to be. Meditate on them until you fall asleep. Look at them until you are dreaming about them. Wake up with them and no demon will stop you from getting there.

KEY THOUGHT

You are rated by your result, not your insult.

God says, '*All the land which thou seest, to thee will I give it....*' (Gen. 13:15). Most of the time, we go to bed in the night thinking of our problems. We sleep depressed; dream oppressed and wake up suppressed and paralysed. What kind of life is that? When your thoughts are focused on where you are in life, your life will confirm that where you are is where you desire to be. '*For as he thinketh in his heart, so is he*' Proverbs 23:7). The Bible says, '*Guard your heart with all diligence for out of it are the issues of life*' (Proverbs 4:23). It has been said that what dominates your mind will direct your life. This is true even in the spiritual realm. Travel away with the wings of your imagination to where you want to be and your life will meet you there.

Remember this: ***you are rated by your result, not your insult.***

COUNSEL

1. Refuse to dwell on your present challenges.
2. Begin to speak out and confess your desired positive expectations.

For Further Understanding, Get This Message: Living With A Vision.

BOOK QUOTE: *When a person sits down doing nothing and is afraid of failing, he will never go forward.* Culled from *10 PRINCIPAL SECRETS OF PRINCIPAL PEOPLE.*

(From Wednesday July 7, 2013)

20

God Believes In You

Behold my servant, whom I uphold; mine elect, in whom my soul delighteth; I have put my spirit upon him: he shall bring forth judgment to the Gentiles. He shall not fail nor be discouraged, till he have set judgment in the earth: and the isles shall wait for his law. **– ISA 42:1,4**

RECENTLY WHILE MEDITATING, I was pondering on the mystery of God's choice of imperfect people to accomplish His purpose. For God to believe that an unstable Simon would become a solid, dependable Peter is amazing. He knew that Peter would deny Him. He knew that Peter would return to his fishing profession after His crucifixion, yet He called him Peter (meaning the 'rock') and destined him to be a pillar of the early Church. He also knew that Peter would repent, get back into the ministry and subsequently die for the sake of the gospel. God believes in you!

The world may judge you based on your present condition but God assesses you based on your future destination. The world sees your container but God watches your intentions. God believes that you will eventually become mature and successful even if you are appearing immature and failing currently. God believes that your current state does not in any way suggest your final outcome. Before God sent the prophet Jonah to Nineveh, God, who knows all things, knew that Jonah would try to resist and go in another direction. But He also knew that Jonah would eventually prophesy to the Ninevites. God believes in you!

The question is 'Do you believe in yourself?' 'Do you believe that no matter where your life is right now, your outcome must be good?' I have realised that people don't fail and end up defeated in life because the devil is too powerful but because of their failure to have faith that God believes in them. Also, they don't believe in themselves. God believes in you. Believe in yourself!

KEY THOUGHT
The world may judge you based on your present condition but God assesses you based on your future destination.

Remember this: ***the world may judge you based on your present condition but God assesses you based on your future destination.***

COUNSEL:

1. Look into the Scripture and find out the promises of God for your life.
2. Begin to believe what God believes about you. Speak them out boldly and take actions where necessary.

For further understanding, get this message: Destined To Excel

BOOK QUOTE ***Your aim in life determines your end in life.*** Culled from *30 SECRETS TO THE TOP* by Dr Paul Enenche.

(From Tuesday, July 30 2013)

21 Issues Have Solutions

There hath no temptation taken you but such as is common to man: but God is faithful, who will not suffer you to be tempted above that ye are able; but will with the temptation also make a way to escape, that ye may be able to bear it. **1 COR. 10:13**

THE ISSUES TROUBLING your life may seem to defy solutions today, but if you persist in your attempt to find lasting solutions, you will eventually get them. My advice is this: TRY AGAIN!

The woman with the issue of blood had tried everything she could to no avail. She decided to try Jesus and solution came. Elijah prayed for rain but it did not come. He prayed again and again until the seventh time, the cloud formed and the rain fell (1 kings 18:42-45). Samson became a prisoner to the Philistines but he called on God again at his death and he killed more Philistines

than he had ever killed before in his lifetime (Judges 16:28-30).

KEY THOUGHT

Until you let go of past failures, you can never lay hold on future success.

Until you let go of past failures, you can never lay hold on future success. Never use your history to predict your destiny; keep trying until that history is rewritten. God will bring an end to the issues that are presently a thorn in your flesh or roadblock on your pathway to destiny, in Jesus' Name.

Remember this: ***until you let go of past failures, you can never lay hold on future success.***

COUNSEL

1. Hold on to the word, prophecies and conviction you have about God and His mercies.
2. See every negative situation as a phase that will soon fade away.

For further understanding, get this message: The End Of The Issue

BOOK QUOTE: ***There is no situation that is beyond solution.*** Culled from *365 WISDOM CAPSULES* by Dr Paul Enenche.

(From Wednesday, 17th November 2010)

22

Take The Battle To The Enemy

***I have fought a good fight, I have finished my course, I have kept the faith.* – 2 TIM 4:7**

THE BATTLES YOU AND your family are faced with currently may be generational in nature. Your ancestors may have been responsible for it and your grandparents may have known little or nothing about the warfare. Therefore, you must make up your mind that it will end with you. You can actually end the battle.

I listened to the story of an African preacher who suddenly divorced his wife after twenty years of marriage. On getting to know about this, Bishop T.D. JAKES told him, '*Well, you can be divorced and may still be a successful preacher, but if you don't reconcile with your wife, you are going to leave the battle for your children to fight. You have to deal with it.*'

> **KEY THOUGHT**
>
> ***If you don't fight, the battle will linger.***

The man of God came back home and decided to look into his family history. It was revealed that in addition to coming from a polygamous home of thirty-five children altogether, he only got to know his father at age seventeen (17). His father was divorced and all his other thirty-four brothers and sisters had either experienced divorce or were separated. His uncles, cousins, and close relations were not left out. He suddenly realised that there was a curse of marital failure in his lineage. He made up his mind to fight it. He reconciled with his wife at that time in order to break the curse. Sadly, the marriage still ended in divorce. I pray that you will not leave any battle behind for your children in Jesus Name. If you don't fight, the battle will linger. Live on the offensive, fight the battle.

Remember this: ***if you don't fight, the battle will linger.***

COUNSEL

1. Do a family history check on your lineage for any negative generational yoke.
2. If there is any, deal with it by the blood of Jesus and the power of the word.

For further understanding, get this message: Dealing With Ancestral Limitations, Establishing Generational Blessing

BOOK QUOTE ***If you do not like the level where you are now, do not fly from there, but fight from there.*** Culled from *30 SECRETS TO THE TOP* by Dr Paul Enenche.

(From Friday, 26th Novemeber 2010)

23

Fact Versus Truth

For we walk by faith, not by sight:
– 2 COR 5:7

THE LITERAL MEANING of the above message is, as Christians, we are meant to operate, make progress and carry out our actions based on truth (which gives birth to faith because God's Word is truth- John 17:17) and not on fact (which is based on sight or the senses).

In one of our previous studies, Peter despised the 'fact', embraced the 'truth,' and got miracles. (Fact was, he toiled all night and caught nothing. Truth was, '*launch out into the deep, and let down your nets for a draught*' – Luke 5:4-5). We must understand that truth is superior to, and stronger than fact. Fact is temporal and changeable but the truth (of God's Word) is eternal and unchangeable. Even history has shown that fact can become untrue (apart from Divine intervention).

For example, it was a fact many years ago that malaria was incurable and many people died because of it, but that is no longer true today. It was agreed as a fact in time past that iron could neither float nor fly. Today, heavy tons of iron in steel form are floating and flying from one part of the world to the other as ships and aircrafts carrying both man and cargo. In those days, there was no drugs for AIDS at all. Today, there are anti-retroviral drugs, enzyme protease inhibitors and others that are used to prolong lives, increase body immunity, and eradicate HIV considerably from the blood stream. If time can alter fact, how much more shall the truth of God's Word destroy fact in an instant? Your outcome is determined by what you believe - fact or truth. Despise the fact and believe the truth.

KEY THOUGHT

Your outcome is determined by what you believe - fact or truth.

Remember this: ***your outcome is determined by what you believe - fact or truth.***

COUNSEL

1. Endeavour to place the Word of God above every situation.

For further understanding, get this message: Your character and your future.

BOOK QUOTE ***You do not maximise your life until you understand the season.*** Culled from *MAKING FULL PROOF OF MINISTRY* by Dr Paul Enenche.

(Saturday, 16th September 2006)

24

The Killer Called Guilt

Then Judas, which had betrayed him, when he saw that he was condemned, repented himself, and brought again the thirty pieces of silver to the chief priests and elders, And he cast down the pieces of silver in the temple, and departed, and went and hanged himself. **– MATT 27:3, 5.**

JUDAS ISCARIOT DIED of guilt. No one shot him; no sickness killed him. Being weighed down by guilt, he took his own life. Guilt is a killer. That is the point! Scriptures make it clear that healing can be delayed and even denied by guilt. '*Confess your faults one to another, and pray one for another that you may be healed*' (James 5:16). Also joy is arrested if guilt is established. David cried out for the restoration of the joy of his salvation when he fell and was guilty (Ps. 51). The entire system: spirit, soul and body comes under tension when guilt is in action. Until your heart is free, your life is not free. You must determine to live a clean, clear life. Don't do things today that will cause guilt and regrets tomorrow. Weigh the long-term consequences

of what you do. You may lie, cheat or kill today and get what you want but in times to come, you will live a life of guilt and regrets. Someone may get what they want through illegal means but a time will come when they will realise that they no longer want what they got because of guilt. In such lives, whenever Divine intervention is sought, satan can use it as a reason why they cannot be helped; then, faith becomes a challenge. Please live your life not only with today in mind tomorrow as well. Whatever it takes to be totally free at heart, do it. Confess your sins to your Maker. Confess your fault to your brothers and sisters in the Lord. Where necessary, give and receive forgiveness and then, life will flow, sin and death will flee.

KEY THOUGHT
The entire system: spirit, soul and body comes under tension when guilt is in action.

Remember this: ***the entire system: spirit, soul and body comes under tension when guilt is in action.***

COUNSEL

1. Read the full account of Judas' and David's guilt (Matt. 27:3-5; Ps. 50:1-13)
2. Draw wisdom lessons from their accounts.
3. Apply these lessons to your life.

For further understanding, get this message: Character And Favour

BOOK QUOTE ***The power of innocence is stronger than the power of experience.*** Culled from *REASON FOR LIVING* by Dr Paul Enenche.

(From Thursday, 25th October, 2012)

25 The Enemy Is Profitable

Go, gather together all the Jews... and fast ye for me,... I also and my maidens will fast likewise;... and if I perish, I perish. **– EST 4:16**

THE ACCOUNT IN OUR anchor text is the word of Esther to Mordecai on the course of action they needed to take concerning the malicious plot of Haman to eliminate the Jews. Is it not true therefore, that your enemy is profitable? Esther, Mordecai and the whole of the Jews would not have thought of praying and fasting at this time if not for the extreme hostility, enmity and animosity of Haman.

The truth is, the real enemy will move you into a place of deeper relationship with God. There are spiritual exercises you won't think of embarking upon if not for an opposition somewhere. It draws you and God closer and increases

your spiritual maturity and stature. You are also ushered into a realm of desperate faith and trust in God; you can't afford to doubt God. **How profitable is the enemy?**

KEY THOUGHT
The real enemy will move you into a place of deeper relationship with God.

The enemy helps you to work on your resolve to succeed in life. It helps you to determine by all means not to fail in life. Queen Esther was ready to embark on the risk of going to see the king without invitation, and she was ready to do that because of the enemy. Enmity pushes you off the life of ease and complacency into a life of risk and adventure. Do you have enemies? If the answer is yes, then move closer in relationship with God. Determine never to fail, and you will profit.

Remember this: ***the real enemy will move you into a place of deeper relationship with God.***

COUNSEL:

1. Meditate on the benefits of the enemy in the second paragraph.
2. Read the entire account of Esther and draw out wisdom lessons to apply.

For further understanding, get this message: Missing Link- Pt 3

BOOK QUOTE: ***It is not everything the enemy is doing against you that is really against you.*** Culled from *365 WISDOM CAPSULES* by Dr Paul Enenche.

(From Friday, 7th November, 2012)

26

The Difference Between Men

And the Lord said unto her, Two nations are in thy womb, and two manner of people shall be separated from thy bowels; and the one people shall be stronger than the other people; and the elder shall serve the younger. – GEN 25:23

THE BIBLE PASSAGE in our anchor text was the reply of God to Rebekah when she was troubled about what was going on in her womb. And it is loaded with revelation.

The first revelation is that people have the potential to become nations. People are the foundation for nations. A person can rise to assume the wealth, power, and influence of nations if he gives life whatever it takes. Bill Gates for example (and the organisation he represents) is heavier than some nations of the world financially.

Secondly, the Word says, '...*two manner of people shall be separated from thy bowels...*' This means that, what separates one person from another is their manners. The difference between people is in their manners, character, principles and practices. What are the practices of your life? That is what will distinguish you on earth.

KEY THOUGHT

The difference between people is in their manners, character, principles and practices.

Remember this: ***the difference between people is their manners, character, principles and practices.***

COUNSEL:

1. Cultivate godly Scriptural principles, manners and character.
2. Do a character study on Daniel and imbibe his character.

For further understanding, get this message: The Principles Of Principal People

BOOK QUOTE: ***Making a difference is more profitable than making a living.*** Culled from *REASON FOR LIVING* by Dr Paul Enenche.

(From Thursday, 4th January, 2007).

27

Surviving Betrayal

And while he yet spake, behold a multitude, and he that was called Judas, one of the twelve, went before them, and drew near unto Jesus to kiss him. But Jesus said unto him, Judas, betrayest thou the Son of man with a kiss? **– LUKE 22:47-48**

BETRAYAL IS SYNONYMOUS with existence. Somebody you trust in one way or the other can betray your trust. God Almighty is not excluded from the list of those who have been betrayed; the trusted Lucifer, the guardian of the throne and the co-ordinator of the other angels betrayed his Master (God). He rebelled, taking 1/3rd of the angels in Heaven with him. Our Lord, Jesus Christ was betrayed by His treasurer, a person of trust. You know, it is not everybody that is appoint-able as treasurer. Treasurers are normally some of the most trusted people in an organisation. That was who Judas was but he betrayed the trust. He (Judas) used a sign of love (kiss) to communicate hate. Judas' kiss meant Jesus' death.

Many times, people have used the kiss to kill. The point is- your best friend can cause you to experience the worst evil ever. People who know your secret might choose to reveal it or use it against you. People who know your standard and principles could deliberately decide to violate them even when you trusted them to respect and venerate them. Note that there is a universal scarcity of people who can be trusted. Don't be too naïve so that you don't fall over and over again as a victim to betrayal.

alpines, où elle peut facilement creuser son gîte et obtenir, tout à la fois, à portée de terrier, son couvert de Graminées, elle sait, à l'occasion, se satisfaire des gros éboulis colonisés par des plages éparses de végétation herbacée. Outre l'intérêt d'une pente pour faciliter la surveillance de l' environnement, celle-ci doit être suffisante pour prévenir également l'inondation du refuge souterrain.

« Gros rongeur » n'est pas une insulte suprême adressée à une Marmotte adulte puisque tête plus corps atteignent cinquante à soixante-dix centimètres de longueur, auxquels il convient d'ajouter quinze à vingt centimètres d'appendice caudal touffu. Chez l'adulte, également, si le poids, début octobre, avant l'entrée en léthargie, accuse cinq à sept kilogrammes, il aura littéralement fondu de moitié au printemps, n'atteignant plus que deux kilogrammes cinq à trois kilogrammes trois au mois d'avril.

La fourrure épaisse de la Marmotte qui la préserve du froid et de la neige toujours possibles, peut revêtir différentes teintes, selon l'âge — plus uniformes et plus grises chez les jeunes de l'année — mais également selon les différentes tribus. Chez ces dernières, on observe des dominances à « manteau » fauve ou roux ; dans d'autres, le pelage présente de larges étendues sombres, presque noires. Ce qui exacerbe le changement apparent de couleur chez un même sujet, lorsqu'il se déplace, c'est la disposition des poils de jarre qui comportent chacun quatre segments colorés : noir, fauve, noir et beige vers l'apex.

Les membres de ce fouisseur expert sont trapus, munis de petites « mains » dont les empreintes, facilement observables sur la neige, trahissent l'existence de quatre doigts griffus aux pattes antérieures, et cinq sur le pied qui est plus long.

La Marmotte possède un œil dont la rétine est exclusivement pourvue de cônes, ce qui la prive de vision crépusculaire, ou au sein de son univers souterrain. En revanche, la disposition latérale de ses globes oculaires lui garantit un champ de vision très large, y compris vers le ciel, d'où la mort peut fondre à tout instant.

Les incisives, à croissance continue, constituent de redoutables ciseaux à bois, bien commodes pour ronger et « cueillir » toutes sortes de friandises végétales. De couleur ivoire, chez les jeunes, les dents paraissent s'enduire de nicotine avec l'âge.

C'est un charmant spectacle d'observer la Marmotte, à quatre pattes, sélectionner délicatement une tendre Fétuque ou déguster le cœur d'un Cirse très épineux, en ponctuant ce repas de hochements de queue. Parfois, elle se campe confortablement sur son derrière, dans une attitude « recueillie », mains jointes sur un Trèfle ou un Lotier particulièrement savoureux. Il est rare d'observer la Marmotte en train de boire, mais ceci ne veut pas dire qu'elle craigne l'eau, puisque j'en ai surpris une, traverser le torrent de la Neuvachette, à partir d'un méandre, avec la complicité du courant. Par contre, j'ai, à deux reprises au moins, découvert, des sujets noyés sur des bordures de lacs, au printemps, au moment de la débâcle de la glace . Peut-être avaient-elles simplement mésestimé la fragilité de la surface et péri d'hydrocution !

Le territoire d'une tribu ou colonie familiale est délimité grâce aux sécrétions des glandes jugales, qui dressent une sorte de barrière olfactive invisible, à l'encontre des Marmottes « étrangères ».

Le plus souvent, lorsqu'un mâle d'une autre colonie pénètre à l'intérieur d'un camp défendu, il en est vertement chassé à grands cris et s'enfuit alors, tout penaud, la queue entre les jambes. J'ai cependant eu l'occasion d'assister à une violation de domicile qui s'est achevée beaucoup plus « tragiquement ». C'était un premier juillet, je devais gagner le refuge de la Valette par le Pas de l'Ane et, en avance sur l'horaire fixé, je fis un détour par le cirque du Petit Marchet. Sur le plateau, en-dessous, quelques Marmottes vaquaient sans tracas à leurs occupations. Brusquement, vers quinze heures, éclatèrent, sur la gauche, des cris provenant de deux individus facilement repérables à leur comportement : ils roulaient tous deux enlacés. Bien vite, je constatais la couleur anormalement rouge qui maculait leurs fourrures ; il fallait se rendre à l'évidence, ce ne pouvait être que du sang ! L'empoignade était entrecoupée de tentatives de fuite effectuées par celle qui semblait la plus petite ; c'était peine perdue, la mêlée reprenait de plus belle. La dégringolade eut lieu sur cent cinquante mètres, durant une douzaine de minutes. L'idée de les séparer m'était venue à l'esprit, mais je me résignais finalement à subir la leçon brutale qui s'offrait à mes yeux.

Peu de cris dans la phase ultime de ce combat, douleur ou rage on ne pouvait le dire ! Pas plus sans doute que la cause exacte de cette lutte : femelle ou territoire ?

La mort allait survenir moins d'un quart d'heure plus tard. Sans une plainte, la vie quittait peu à peu ce corps déchiré, les muscles se relâchèrent, entraînant une dernière roulade. Apparurent alors griffes et dents acérées et rougies, dont j'apprenais tristement l'usage, autre que la cueillette des fleurs.

Une telle agressivité, entre Marmottes, est sans doute exceptionnelle, mais elle peut, par contre, leur sauver la vie face au chien domestique ou au Renard qui ne les aura pas saisis, à la nuque, immédiatement.

Cependant revenons à la colonie qui se compose d'une dizaine d'individus, répartis selon un schéma bien défini, comme l'a observé le chercheur Américain David Barash, au cours de ses études conduites en Haute Maurienne.

Après avoir capturé et marqué, à l'aide de peinture et de marques aux oreilles, la totalité des sujets de quatre colonies, à proximité des refuges du Vallon, du Mollard, du Cuchet et du Carro, il décrivit le modèle familial qui comporte : un mâle adulte, rarement deux, une ou deux femelles adultes, ainsi que les jeunes de l'année précédente, au nombre de trois en moyenne et enfin l'ensemble des Marmottons de l'année : de deux à cinq.
Alors que toute la famille occupe, durant l'hibernation, le même terrier — celui-ci offre l'entrée la plus grande : trente-six centimètres de diamètre en moyenne mais aussi la plus sale — à la belle saison, le mâle adulte habite solitaire, un terrier situé à une centaine de mètres à l'écart et à une vingtaine de mètres plus haut en altitude. L'une des femelles en gestation continue de résider dans le terrier d'hibernation pendant l'été, alors que la seconde, gestante ou non, s'approprie un terrier distant de quinze à vingt mètres du premier. Les jeunes de l'année précédente, quant à eux, occupent un terrier simple dans un rayon de vingt mètres ; c'est seulement à l'issue de la seconde année qu'ils seront contraints de se disperser et d'aller, ailleurs, chercher « fortune ».

Grâce aux marques distinctives apposées aux animaux, D. Barash a pu apprécier l'évolution des comportements sociaux au cours de la période estivale dans chacune des colonies.

Les différences individuelles de comportement : d'accueil, de jeu-combat et de poursuite agressive, se sont révélées plus accentuées chez les adultes que parmi les individus d'un an et, également, plus marquées, pour les mêmes classes d'âge et de sexe, entre les quatre colonies qu'au sein d'un même groupe familial. Par ailleurs, ces comportements de « civilité », ludique et d'agressivité, ont tendance à s'estomper au fur et à mesure que s'écoulent les beaux jours.

Nous sommes maintenant fin septembre, la montagne est revêtue de ses plus beaux contrastes, elle exhale ses senteurs les plus sauvages. Je me dirige vers le refuge de la Femma, les glaciers des Roches Blanches éclaboussent de pureté le ciel marine. En chemin, j'éprouve le sentiment de traverser une contrée peuplée de Marmottes indifférentes à ma visite, toutes accaparées qu'elles sont, par les travaux de fenaison. L'une d'elle galope sous mes pieds, une brassée d'herbe dans la gueule comme parée d' une énorme moustache fauve ; c'est qu'il est grand temps maintenant de se préparer à passer six mois sous terre !

Ce foin n'est pas destiné à être consommé, mais à tapisser la litière du nid d'hibernation de la famille, situé à deux mètres sous terre, à l'extrémité d'une galerie pouvant atteindre une dizaine de mètres de longueur.

Le terrier étant finalement coupé de l'extérieur par un tampon de terre d'un ou deux mètres, la longue, très longue nuit d'hiver va pouvoir commencer ; chaque individu s'assoupissant de plus en plus profondément, roulé en boule. La température de leur corps suit, à un ou deux degrés supérieurs près, celle du milieu ambiant, leur rythme respiratoire se ralentit jusqu'à une seule inspiration par minute vers 6° C, celui du cœur tombe à environ vingt-cinq systoles par minute contre soixante-quinze ordinairement.

Les Marmottes ne se réveilleront qu'une fois par mois environ afin d'évacuer, dans une antichambre du terrier, les déchets du métabolisme sous forme d'excréments.

C'est finalement l'épuisement total des réserves de graisse qui les contraindra à mettre le bout du nez dehors, au printemps, même si la neige et le froid persistent au dehors. Il est en effet impérieux, pour elles, de recouvrer des forces quels que soient les risques encourus, en traversant un champ de neige pour grignoter un maigre paillasson d'herbes sèches !

Il est certain que c'est à cette époque que l'Aigle royal, l'ennemi héréditaire, qui va avoir à nourrir, à l'aire, un ou deux « roitelets », va le plus « ponctionner » cette proie combien rentable !

Plus que la chasse à l'affût, pratiquée par certains montagnards dissimulés derrière une meurtrière de cailloux, c'est le braconnage au chien et surtout le « piochage » des terriers d'hibernation qui sont pavenus à vider ces sympathiques « siffleux », comme les nomment si bien les canadiens, de montagnes entières.

Les seuls griefs que l'on puisse reprocher aux Marmottes, ce que ne manquent pas de faire des agriculteurs de Haute-Maurienne, à Bonneval ou à Termignon, c'est de sortir des matériaux de leur terrier, lesquels entravent l'exploitation des alpages, voire déteriorent les engins de fauche. A cela, le Parc de la Vanoise a, jusqu'alors, administré un seul remède : l'arrestation pure et simple des Rongeurs jugés indésirables et leur exil dans des contrées où ils étaient, au contraire, ardemment souhaités. C'est ainsi que sur les Hauts plateaux du Vercors, par exemple, vous pourrez désormais entendre siffler, avec un petit accent savoyard, des Marmottes, toutes « heureuses » de recoloniser leurs territoires d'antan.

La Bartavelle

"C'étaient des perdrix, mais leur poids me surprit : elles étaient aussi grandes que des coqs de basse-cour, et j'avais beau hausser les bras, leurs becs rouges touchaient encore le gravier.
Alors, mon cœur sauta dans ma poitrine : des Bartavelles ! Des Perdrix Royales !... Je haussais vers le ciel la gloire de mon père en face du soleil couchant".

Qui ne s'est délecté à la lecture de cette apothéose de l'un des plus célèbres souvenirs d'enfance de Marcel Pagnol ? Aussi, ce n'est pas sans scrupule que j'ai essayé de confronter quelques-uns des détails fournis par notre sympathique académicien à ceux, tout-à-fait insipides, des traités modernes de zoologie.

S'il est parfaitement exact que la Perdrix bartavelle ou Perdrix grecque est la plus grande de toutes, il est curieux que les quelques années qui nous séparent de ce récit aient, à ce point, affecté le poids de ces oiseaux qui, de un kilo et demi à l'époque, pour le mâle, s'établit aujourd'hui, au maximum, à sept cent cinquante grammes. Il en va de même de la femelle qui, de un kilo deux cent cinquante grammes, est tombée de nos jours, dans le meilleur des cas, à six cent cinquante grammes. Peut-être était-ce simplement la balance de l'épicier qui "faussait", à moins que cela confirme les dires de certains chasseurs qui, "dans le temps", tiraient des gibiers gros comme ça ! Ceci avant notre ère de la consanguinité et de la dégénérescence... !

Je préfère, pour ma part, mettre ce "glissement morphologique" sur le compte de l'accent méridional au même titre que celui de la taille qui, toujours, à en croire les manuels "sans thym ni laurier" accordent à Alectoris graeca saxatilis (Bechstein 1805) de trente-huit à quarante-deux centimètres.

Il n'en reste pas moins que la Bartavelle est une espèce à répartition géographique limitée, tant en Europe qu'en France, où elle se confine pratiquement aux Alpes internes avec un accroissement des effectifs du Nord au Sud.

Dans notre département, c'est seulement en Maurienne qu'elle peut être considérée comme relativement bien représentée. Je l'ai cependant encore notée récemment dans des vallées de Tarentaise, aussi peu favorables a priori que celle de Champagny-en-Vanoise.

Outre son extension géographique limitée, les effectifs de cette espèce sont considérés comme étant, à nouveau, en régression ces dernières années. Une première diminution notable avait, en effet, été constatée au début du siècle. Parmi les raisons invoquées pour expliquer ce déclin de la Bartavelle, on retient notamment : les modifications climatiques — les printemps et étés pluvieux pénalisant sa reproduction — et, par ailleurs, l'abandon de certaines pratiques agricoles de montagne, comme la culture du Seigle ou de l'Avoine, qui priverait cet oiseau d'une importante nourriture d'appoint à la mauvaise saison.

Bien qu'inféodée aux étages subalpins et alpins, la Bartavelle, contrairement au Lagopède et au Tétras-lyre, est peu adaptée à résister aux forts enneigements.

En effet, à la différence de ces deux "cousins", elle ne possède pas de pattes emplumées ou pectinées qui lui facilitent ses déplacements à la surface du manteau neigeux, elle ne creuse pas non plus d'igloos qui lui permettent de résister aux déperditions importantes de température ; enfin, elle ne s'alimente pas à partir d'espèce ligneuse accessible comme l'Aulne vert.

De par cette inadéquation aux conditions hivernales, la Bartavelle est contrainte d'effectuer des déplacements saisonniers altitudinaux.

C'est ainsi que l'été, elle fréquente, en couple, parfois jusque vers trois mille mètres, les éboulis rocheux, colonisés par des touffes de végétation herbacée, exposée au Sud et à l'Est. Les banquettes rocheuses du Mont de la Para, au-dessus d'Entre deux Eaux, visualisent bien ce type de milieu. A l'automne, on voit se former des rassemblements et dès les premières neiges, les Bartavelles gagnent des lieux plus hospitaliers, comme par exemple, la proximité du village de Bessans vers dix sept cents mètres.

Aire limitée, effectifs réduits, mœurs discrètes en dehors des parades, tout concourt à rehausser le caractère "glorieux" de l'oiseau. Ceci explique qu'il me soit arrivé de participer à une "traque" à la Perdrix Royale pour le compte d'un ornithologue, spécialiste des œufs, auteur d'ouvrages de renommée internationale. Ce naturaliste avait, au cours de sa carrière, eu l'occasion d'observer, sur les cinq continents, plus de mille espèces d'oiseaux, eh bien, le croiriez-vous ? Il manquait à son palmarès : la Perdrix bartavelle.

C'est en ces circonstances qu'il nous échut à Henri Gonthier, Hubert Tournier et moi-même, le rôle délicat de chien de chasse sur les contreforts de la vallée d'Averolle.

How do you respond to betrayal? First, understand that human beings are capable of anything. To expect perfection from man is to end in frustration. Give allowance for failures, mistakes, errors, disappointments, betrayals and weaknesses so that you don't get too surprised and shocked when someone else fails. Next, deepen your trust, confidence, and relationship with God. He never fails. For every betrayal, your relationship with God should become stronger, and then you will become more sensitive and resistant to betrayal and deception. Finally, try again because there are those who will not fail you, and God will bring them your way. For every Naomi, there is a Ruth and for every David, there is a Jonathan, who can be trusted to the end.

KEY THOUGHT

To expect perfection from man is to end in frustration.

Remember this: ***to expect perfection from man is to end in frustration.***

COUNSEL:

1. On your part, do not betray anybody and do not contribute to betraying anyone.
2. Call up somebody and tell them that you forgive their betrayal.

For further understanding, get this message: Your Character And Your Future

BOOK QUOTE: ***To mourn the past is to lose the joy of the future.*** Culled from *30 SECRETS TO THE TOP* by Dr Paul Enenche.

(From Saturday, 17th November, 2012)

28

Christianity Is Not Mediocrity

Arise, shine; for thy light is come, and the glory of the Lord is risen upon thee. – ISA 60:1

IN THE DAYS OF OLD, it appeared as if Christianity meant mediocrity. A man of God who has been in ministry for almost 40 years now once said that about 35 years ago, when there was an outburst of revival in Nigeria, there were things Christians were not permitted to buy. For example, if you wanted to buy a bicycle, you would not buy the shiny type because it was seen as a mark of worldliness. If you wanted to buy meat, you would buy the inferior, low-grade type called 'kpomo' (cowhide or skin). You wouldn't buy normal body cream but only petroleum jelly so that flies can be perching on you anywhere you go. You couldn't wear a tie to look decent and call yourself a Christian. All these were satanic advertisement of mediocrity.

The devil wanted to equate Christianity with mediocrity and poverty. In those days, the poorer you were as a Christian, the better. They used to say, 'As poor as the Church rat', because the rats inside the Church had no food to eat.

KEY THOUGHT
God is a God of excellence and we are created in His image and excellence.

But there is already a turnaround in the Church today! God is never excited about mediocrity. God is a God of excellence and we are created in His image of excellence. Let us arise and be like God in excellence. Let us shine for His light has come and His glory is risen upon us. Though darkness covers the earth, the Lord will rise upon us and His glory will be seen in our lives (Is. 60:1).

Remember this: ***God is the God of excellence and we are created in His image of excellence.***

COUNSEL:

1. Ask God to increase the revelation of His glory in your life and on the Church.
2. Determine never to equate Christianity with poverty or mediocrity. Refuse to be a mediocre

For further understanding, get this message: Destined To Excel

BOOK QUOTE ***You misrepresent God when you act in mediocrity.*** Culled from *365 WISDOM CAPSULES* by Dr Paul Enenche.

(From Saturday, 3rd August 2013)

29

Fire For Fire

And when they had prayed, the place was shaken where they were assembled together; and they were all filled with the Holy Ghost, and they spake the word of God with boldness. – ACTS 4:31

NEVER ALLOW THE devil to drown your voice. Never allow your voice to be drowned at the place of prayer because of any threat, challenge or pressure. Never allow the enemy to reduce your prayer life. Don't allow a delay in your expectations, a conspiracy in the office or any demon or witch to reduce your prayer life. Never reduce your commitment to fellowship and evangelism. Never allow any devil to tame you like a tamed lion that behaves like a dog. Never allow any devil to cage you, your destiny or your voice.

What then do you do in the season of pressure? Increase your spiritual pressure because it is pressure that handles pressure. Positive pressure handles negative pressure.

Increase your pressure of prayer, worship and the study of the Word. Increase your pressure of fellowship and waiting on the Lord. When two pressures meet each other, the higher pressure will cause the lower pressure to bow.

KEY THOUGHT

Positive pressure handles negative pressure.

I heard some time ago that the best way to handle a raging forest fire in ancient times was to set a control fire from another angle. The control fire had a limit that could be controlled and it will begin to burn and move in the direction of the fire that is burning uncontrollably. The place where the two fires meet is the end of both fires.

It takes fire to fight fire. It takes Holy Ghost fire to arrest hell fire. It takes the fire of the spirit to arrest the fire of the flesh. If you can make up your mind that no devil is going to reduce your fire, then you are going to send the devil and his agents back to hell.

Remember this: ***positive pressure handles negative pressure.***

COUNSEL

1. Be prayerful.
2. Never give the devil any room in your life.

For further understanding, get this message: In The Days Of His Power -pt 3

BOOK QUOTE ***We must match force with force, fire with fire, and raise the banner of God's power thousands of times over the activities of satan.*** Culled from *THOU ART MY BATTLE AXE* by Dr. Paul Enenche.

(From Wednesday, 4th September 2013)

30

The devil Is An Errand Boy

And we know that all things work together for good to them that love God, to them who are the called according to his purpose. **– ROMANS 8:28**

PONTIUS PILATE AND all the people who crucified Jesus Christ (including the demons) thought that what they were doing to Jesus was what they had planned to do but the Bible says that what they were doing was only '*Whatsoever God's hand and counsel determined before to be done...*' (Acts 4:28 paraphrased). The devil is an errand boy and messenger. He is running God's errand without his own knowledge or permission. For Calvary to happen, God seem to have said, 'I need my Son to die; Satan help me achieve it. Go ahead; do the assignment.' This means that Satan does not have the right of action in the life of a child of God. Even before he attacked Job, he had to secure God's permission.

The devil's work in many people's lives is only a part of God's

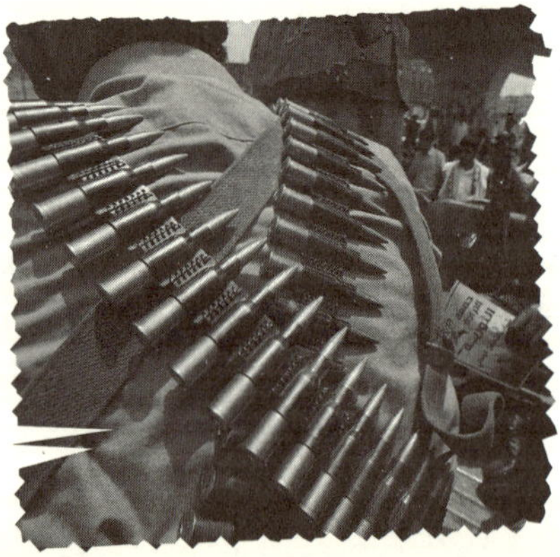

process. God is doing a bigger work, because *'All things work together for good to them that love God; even to them that are the called according to his purpose'* (Romans 8:28). A day will come when you will look for the devil to see whether you can thank him for how much he assisted you to reach your destiny and for helping you become more prayerful and anointed.

KEY THOUGHT

The devil's work in many people's lives is only a part of God's process.

Don't over celebrate or over empower the devil. Some people scream 'Blood of Jesus,' at the sight of even cockroach or lizard. The devil does not have the license to do whatever he feels like in the life of an authentic, 'brutalous,' ferocious, audacious, firebrand, rugged, brutal, tongue-talking, devil-chasing, fire-spitting, red-eyed and spirit-filled child of God.

Remember this: ***the devil's work in many people's lives is only a part of God's process.***

COUNSEL

1. Do not give the devil unnecessary attention.
2. Always remember that in Christ, you are seated far above principalities and powers.

For further understanding, get this message: Passing From Pressure To Power

BOOK QUOTE: *Do not allow any devil to pocket your destiny because you are unable to grasp where you are going.* Culled from *15 KINGDOM STRATEGIES FOR SURVIVAL* by Dr Paul Enenche.

(From Tuesday, 10th September 2012)

31

Depression Kills

Although the fig tree shall not blossom, neither shall fruit be in the vines, the labour of the Olives shall fail, and the field shall yield no meat, the flock shall be cut off from the fold, and there shall be no herd in the stalls: yet I will rejoice in the Lord, I will joy in the God of my salvation. The Lord God is my strength... **HAB. 3:17-19**

DEPRESSION IS A BASIS of destruction in life because it has the capacity to kill. And what you do not kill can kill you. You must make the choice to always be joyful because life has no spare part. Do not live carelessly and 'depressingly' because you do not have a second opportunity to live. Don't allow any man, woman or devil to frustrate the life that you have.

You see, many people live as if they have a spare life. The fact is, when a day passes, it has already passed away forever. Abraham Lincoln once said, 'Anybody can be as happy as he decides to be'. You know there are people that nothing can ever make happy. Even when you crack the funniest of jokes, they will just be moping at you. Please don't do yourself such a disservice. Don't abuse your own life. It is not profitable to do that. And you know what? Depression is a choice. Joy also is a choice Even if there were circumstances surrounding your birth that are contrary to your life, you still have a choice in the matter. I personally have made up my mind that my joy shall not be based on a bank account, man, Church, house, employment, fashion or car. My joy is in the Lord God Almighty! You see, when your joy is attached to a thing and that thing is attacked, your joy has been automatically attacked. Let God be the source of your joy. Since God cannot be attacked, your joy can never be attacked.

KEY THOUGHT

You need more muscles to frown than to smile.

Depression can never give you anything but destruction and devastation. You can never come to a point where you were so depressed that it aided you in getting the right results, finding a husband, job or getting pregnant. Some medical experts actually found out that you need more muscles to frown than to smile; the muscles you need to frown are said to be almost 4 times the number of muscles you need to smile. Frowning and depression are energy-consuming activities because the contraction of muscle requires energy. Please by all means, avoid the way of depression.

Remember this: ***you need more muscles to frown than to smile.***

COUNSEL

1. Never allow your joy to be dependent on anything or anyone.

For further understanding get this message: Joy For The Top - Pt .5

BOOK QUOTE ***When you are depressed, your mind is blocked, your ears are blocked, and your spirit is blocked.*** Culled from *30 SECRETS TO THE TOP* by Dr Paul Enenche.

(From Friday, 27th September, 2013)

32

Hard Work: The Door To The High Place

Seest thou a man diligent in his business? He shall stand before kings; he shall not stand before mean men – PROV. 22:29

IN THIS WORLD, people may live together but eventually end differently. We don't end at the same place in life because we don't do the same things. There was a notable female Nigerian bank executive who has a twin sister and while she took her place up in life, her twin sister faded off in obscurity. It is not because God is partial or that He loves one person and hates the other. Esau and Jacob for instance did not end in the same place because their mind-sets and lifestyles were different. Your input into your life and assignment will ultimately determine your influence on earth.

People's input into life will determine their influence in life. Your input will determine your impact and outcome. Attention to assignment equals distinction in destiny because life is a fertile ground and man will reap what he sows. How you work today determines where you will stand and the company you will keep tomorrow. The low places of the earth will be history if everybody in this world can have a rugged training in diligence. Hard work is the door to high places. Determine to make hard-work your life's identity.

KEY THOUGHT

Your input will determine your impact and outcome.

Remember this: ***your input will determine your impact and outcome.***

COUNSEL:

1. Make up your mind to avoid slothfulness in all your endeavours.
2. Make sure that you have a schedule of what you want to achieve for each day.

For further understanding get this message: Diligence

BOOK QUOTE: ***Your work determines your worth.*** Culled from *30 SECRETS TO THE TOP* by Dr Paul Enenche.

(From Friday, 13th September, 2013)

33

Be Loaded With The Word

***This book of the law shall not depart out of thy mouth; but thou shalt meditate therein day and night, that thou mayest observe to do according to all that is written therein: for then thou shalt make thy way prosperous, and then thou shalt have good success.* — JOSHUA 1:8**

EXIST AS A WORD-LOADED child of God because until you are fully loaded, you don't download readily. It is 'loadation' that determines 'off loadation'. What fills your heart is what will flow out of your life when you are under pressure. For instance, can oil come out of a sponge that was soaked inside water when it is pressed or put under pressure? No. Is there any amount of beating that will make someone who ate *garri (*Cassava meal) in the morning to vomit rice in the afternoon? (Except you want to kill that person because he cannot bring out what he has not taken in). Many times, pressure comes to reveal content. Every time pressure comes against your life, what fills your heart will flow through your life to confront the pressure and that will determine both your destiny and the destiny of that challenge.

The fact however is, the pressures of life do not serve notice. So what are you stuffing your spirit with? For some people, it is home movies from morning till night and for others, it is football or aimless computer games. Will home movies handle ritual killers? A military personnel does not load his GPMG (General purpose machine gun) when he sights a criminal. The man who is trying to load his weapon when killers arrive is the man who has prepared to die.

KEY THOUGHT

It is 'loadation' that determines 'off-loadation.'

Do not wait for problems or bad dreams to get ready. Stuff your spirit with the Word of God at ordinary times and you cannot be taken by surprise in times of challenge. Some people begin training for Olympic Games four years ahead of time (at the end of the previous Olympic Games). If that could be done to be prepared for physical conflicts, how much more prepared should we be for spiritual conflicts? Take time to continually load your spirit and study Scriptures. To move about without a copy of the Bible in your possession makes you improperly dressed or ill-equipped. It is well!

Remember this: ***it is 'loadation' that determines 'off loadation'***.

COUNSEL

1. Make sure that you have a Bible reading plan such as the one in Seeds of Destiny Bible reading plan.
2. Take out time to meditate on the Word of God.

For further understanding get this message: Passing From Pressure To Power

BOOK QUOTE: ***There is a word from God you will establish in your spirit and it becomes a shield.*** Culled from *15 KINGDOM STRATEGIES FOR SURVIVAL* by Dr Paul Enenche

(From Thursday, 12th Septemebr, 2013)

34

Diligence Is The Cure For Obscurity

Be thou diligent to know the state of thy flocks, and look well to thy herd **– PROVERBS 27:23**

A DILIGENT MAN or woman cannot be hidden or covered. No witch or wizard can cover his or her destiny. I remember the story of a young lady who was trusting God for a husband. She was a very spiritual, hardworking medical doctor. She had a car and was very comfortable but had no husband. She bought a shirt for her prospective husband and hung it in her wardrobe (a prophetic action saying, 'My husband, your shirt is waiting. When will you wear it?') She travelled to London for a wedding and even with the degree, money and everything she had, she was in the kitchen running errands, washing the plates and doing chores. A man who also left Nigeria for that wedding saw her, called the host and asked, 'Who is that lady?' The host replied, 'She is one of our sisters; she came from Nigeria for this occasion.' He then said, 'I have found my wife.' She wasn't doing eye service. She was real. And diligence stood her out. Diligence wiped out her reproach of singleness. Diligence stood her out. Truth is, you can't be diligent and be obscure. And diligent people can't avoid hard work. Work is the hobby of diligent people. For some other people however, computer games, watching movies, etc are their hobbies. When a man is diligent however, work is his joy. It seems as if a 'workworm' bit him.

> **KEY THOUGHT**
>
> ***A diligent man or woman cannot be hidden.***

Personally, I am not afraid for my future if Jesus Christ tarries. By the mercies of God, any work that I do, even if I was coordinating the sweeping of streets, I would not beg because I put in my all into anything I do. You see, when you do average things, you will end up with an average life. Normal people work 8.00am -5.00pm, which is why they are average people. Over 90% of human beings go to work in the morning at 8 or 9 o' clock, and when they close from work, they will do nothing meaningful with their lives until the next day. That is why they dwell in the realm of average. They are living to pay bills for services, fuel the car and have a house to live in; that is an average life. But you can do better than that. You can rise into eminence if you are diligent.

Remember this: ***a diligent man or woman cannot be hidden.***

COUNSEL:

1. Critically evaluate your life to find out if you are a diligent person or not.
2. Make an effort to be more diligent in all you do. Totally avoid the lifestyle of ease and complacence.

For further understanding get this message: Diligence

BOOK QUOTE: ***The higher you want to fly in life, the harder you will have to work.*** Culled from *30 SECRETS TO THE TOP* by Dr Paul Enenche

(From Saturday, 14 September, 201)

35

Power In The Beauty Of Holiness

'O worship the Lord in the beauty of holiness: fear before him, all the earth. – **PSALM 96:9**

PEOPLE WHO MANIFEST GOD'S Power are people who walk in holiness. Beauty of holiness in our anchor text suggests that holiness is a dress. The Bible in Basic English says ' *o give worship to the Lord in holy robes; be in fear before him, all the earth* (Psalm 96:9). Holiness is a robe, garment or apparel and it is spiritually perceivable.

When Elisha used to pass through Shunem, a great woman usually fed him. One day she said to her husband, '*Behold, now I perceive that this is an holy man of God, which passeth by us continually*' (2 Kings 4:9). Who told the Shunamite woman that Elisha was a holy man of God? Nobody; she perceived it.

> **KEY THOUGHT**
>
> ***Holiness is a dress.***

Perception means recognition by knowledge or experience. Do you need anybody to advertise a nurse to you when you see one? No! When you see a policeman with his AK 47 rifle, do you need any advertisement? When you see a senior military officer with stars on his shoulder and medals on his chest, do you need anybody to advertise him to you? When you see a madman, do you need anybody to tell you that he is insane? The dress of the mechanic may be painted with engine oil but he is fully sane and might have millions in his bank account.

In the same manner, every time people encounter you, something is perceived in the spirit realm. Holiness cannot be hidden. The question is, what is the perception in the realm of the spirit concerning your life? What is the perception of your generation? Are you wearing the garment of holiness? It requires the grace of the Lord to so.

Remember this: ***holiness is a dress.***

COUNSEL

1. Live a life of holiness and purity.

For further understanding get this message: Passing From Pressure To Power.

BOOK QUOTE ***Your stand with God at the place of prayer affects your stand in life.*** Culled from *30 SECRETS TO THE TOP* by Dr Paul Enenche

(From Saturday, 7 September, 2013)

36

Weight Is The Enemy Of Flight

Although the fig tree shall not blossom, neither shall fruit be in the vines, the labour of the Olives shall fail, and the field shall yield no meat, the flock shall be cut off from the fold, and there shall be no herd in the stalls: yet I will rejoice in the Lord, I will joy in the God of my salvation. The Lord God is my strength… – Hab. 3:17-19

PEOPLE GO UP when they cheer up and go down when they feel down. Joy is the vehicle that takes a man to the top. Joy is also the flight you take to the high places of the earth.

Joy took Nehemiah to the palace and kept him there. Joy also took David and Joseph to the palace. When you are weighed down, you remain down. Anything that weighs you down is calculated to keep you down. You can't fly high as long as you feel low. Weight is the enemy of flight. The heavier your weight, the more impossible your flight will be.

FACES OF BROKEN BARRENESS

Sister Amaka and Lovelyn had trusted God for the fruit of the womb without headway. Amaka especially had been barren for six years but as she came to Dunamis int'l Gospel Centre, the yoke was broken.

Lovelyn also came to the Church in similar situation, but in July 2013 during the birthday of Dr (Pst) Paul Enenche, she came with an expectation primarily to participate in the birthday cake, but she heard a brutal declaration from God's servant, Dr Paul Enenche, that whoever was trusting God for the fruit of the womb or whatever miracle should claim the miracle. After that day, sister Lovelyn had an encounter in a dream in which God's handmaiden, Dr (Mrs) Becky Enenche handed her a baby boy and prayed for her. The following month, August, 2013, the dream became real. Lovelyn conceived and she is here heavily loaded to the glory of God. – **SOD**

CAREER BREAKTHROUGH AFTER TWENTY FOUR (24) YEARS

I have been a Barristor at Law for twenty four years but was struggling to feed; I was feeding from hand to mouth. In January 2013, I decided to join Dunamis Commission in that condition and God took away my reproach. I am now a legal consultant to many Federal government agencies including the office of the Attorney General of the Federation of Nigeria. God has turned my story around in just six months. Surely God is here. I return all glory to Him. – **Bro. Julius**

MINISTRY TURNED AROUND AFTER AN ENCOUNTER

I had been in ministry for a few years now with a yoke of stagnation in membership strength. Our church membership was never more than forty (40) people. However, this year, I had an encounter with the senior pastor of this Commission, Dr (Pst) Paul Enenche in a dream. He took me straight to my maternal home in our village and prayed for me for about fifteen minutes after which he advised me to follow him so he could show me how to run the ministry in success.

After waking up the following day, I headed straight to Abuja all the way from Kogi State, Nigeria. I slept by the gate of Dunamis Church in Abuja, and I had another revelation where a young man was distributing some materials and also gave me one with a bible passage to read.

The following day after the healing and deliverance service with Dr Enenche, I went back to my base in Kogi state. Brethren, our next church meeting was an explosion. From the membership of forty (40) people, we increased to one hundred and forty (140) and from that number we are now have membership strength of one hundred and eighty people within just two months. I came back to acknowledge the God at work in Dunamis Int'l Gospel Centre. **– Pst. Mark**

A SHOE MANTLE CHANGED MY LIFE

My life was everything but good before my encounter with God's handmaiden, Dr (Mrs) Becky Enenche. On that fateful day, I just joined a group of testifiers to share a testimony over a headache that God healed me of. After the testimony, as I was going back to the pew, Mummy called me and by Divine orchestration, handed me a pair of shoes. When I stepped into the shoes, my life began to attract favour on high frequency. First of all, God gave me a bank job without stress. After a while I was made a branch manager of the branch. As I am talking to you now, I just rounded off a professional examination which is expected to further boost my career in the banking industry. I return to give God the praise. **– Sister Vivian**

ZERO SPERM COUNTS YET TWINS

No verdict is final, including medical verdicts. We serve a God that makes impossibilities to be possible. Many of you seated in front pew of Dunamis headquarters know me as a front-seater at every given service. I was actually confronted with barrenness that lasted for four years after I wedded my husband in 2010. We have been to hospitals and taken all manner of treatment to no avail. After a series of test and diagnosis, my husband was said to have zero sperm count and unfit to impregnate a woman. We decided to cultivate a rigid dedication and commitment to the God that is at work here. God's servant had severally ministered to my husband and I to break the yoke of barrenness, and for a while, it looked like nothing was actually changing but we remained established until today. Evidence is the end of argument; he has given us a testimony to his own glory. – **Sister Chukwurah**

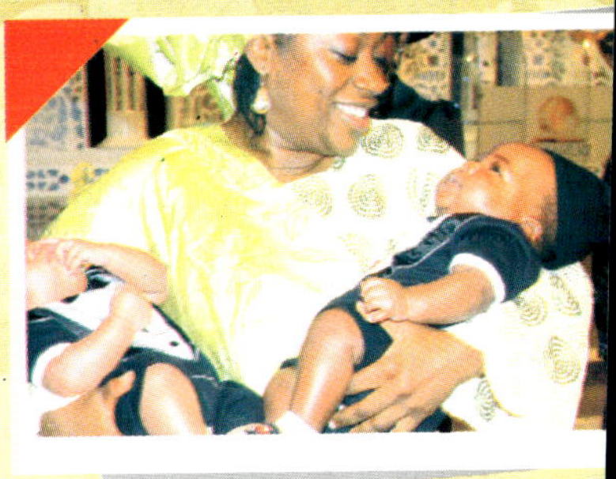

BEDWETTING ARRESTED

Three of my children were seriously bedwetting. These were not infants but children between the ages of four and ten years. The matter became a serious concern to us having done everything necessary as a medical doctor to no avail. I decided to bring three of them to church when I heard a similar testimony shared here. After they encountered the God at work in this commission, they stopped bedwetting. In addition, one of them (my children) who also had an eye problem that necessitated the use of medicated glasses has now been healed by God miraculously. In my own case, I stopped menstruating suddenly without a known cause for a long time, but after I had an encounter with God in a dream with the face of our senior pastor, the next day, my menses returned. I have come to appreciate God for these miracles in my family. **– Sister M**

RAISED FROM DEATH

I was in a certain affliction in which my lap down to the waist was totally engulfed in pains for three weeks before I eventually passed on to eternity. In fact, if it were when I was still in the other religion, I would have been buried within the period, but as a Christian, arrangement for my burial was still on before I jerked back to life.

While on the other side (during the period I was dead), I had crossed the first gate and came to the second gate, before I heard the voice of our pastor, Dr Paul Enenche and the voice said: **"everybody stand up on your feet and shout a loud haliluyah".** Then I sneezed and sat up. Mourners and sympathizers were amazed that a person could be medically confirmed dead for three hours and still live again. Medically speaking, even if a person dead for such duration comes back to life either the brain, the eye or the ear would be inactive or dead. But in my case because of divine intervention, I came out completely perfect. I am healthy today and sound to the glory of God. – **Sister Ibrahim**

BLINDNESS HEALED

I had an accident last year that resulted in the blindness of my left eye. If you take a close look at the eye, you would see some blood stain in the cornea of the eye. I could not see with it before now. On the first day of the **Deborah generation women conference,** as Dr (Mrs) Becky Enenche started the healing ministration, casting out the spirits of blindness, suddenly I discovered that the hitherto blind eye could see very clearly. I can see now! – **Sister J**

HEALED OF CERVICAL CANCER

I came from Bauchi State Nigeria with a terrible diagnosis of a cervical cancer. I had taken all manner of medications from different hospitals but there was no solution. So, I came here for the Healing and Deliverance service in the previous Tuesday, and God's servant Dr Paul Enenche, made some declarations against deadly diseases. At the instance of the word, I proceeded for another test where I was diagnosed cancer-free, and all the associated pains have left me since that day until now and forever in Jesus' name. – **Sister Rehila**

I challenge and encourage you to kill every form of depression in your life. The word 'depression' also means the action of lowering something or pressing something down. Depression is the opposite of elevation. A life of depression keeps people in the valley, while a life of excitement takes people to the mountain. Depression keeps you in the pit but excitement takes you to the top. It is a matter of choice.

> **KEY THOUGHT**
> ***Anything that weighs you down is calculated to keep you down***

Make up your mind today to ruin or deal with everything that is fighting your joy because your joy determines your strength, wisdom, favour and anointing.

Remember this: ***anything that weighs you down is calculated to keep you down.***

COUNSEL:

1. Do everything possible to maintain the joy of the Lord in your life.
2. Dwell in God's Presence habitually.

For further understanding get this message: Joy For The Top - Part 2

BOOK QUOTE: ***When you begin to enjoy sin, God turns His eyes away from you.*** Culled from *15 KINGDOM STRATEGIES FOR SURVIVAL* by Dr Paul Enenche

(From Sunday, 1st September 2013)

37

Issues Are Universal

'There hath no temptation taken you but such as is common to man: but God is faithful, who will not suffer you to be tempted above that ye are able; but will with the temptation also make a way to escape, that ye may be able to bear it'. – 1 COR. 10:13

SATAN IS ALWAYS TRYING to make people believe that they are alone in their predicaments. Many times, all he does is to make people feel that no one else is going through the same kind of problem they are going through. But this is not true! A wise man once said, 'problems are not prejudiced'.

A careful look at Bible characters shows that many of them had issues in their lives. But in spite of those personal issues that challenged their lives and destinies, many of them are today referred to as heroes and heroines of faith.

No matter what you are going through, you are not alone in it. It is interesting to know that the bible refers to your condition as 'common'. If it is common, it can be conquered. All you have to do is to see it as something you can conquer. It has an expiry date; it is not permanent. The scripture declares, '*For surely there is an end; and thine expectation shall not be cut off*' (Proverbs 23:18). Always remember that someone somewhere once confronted and conquered whatever you are currently confronting and your case shall not be different in Jesus Name.

> **KEY THOUGHT**
> ***No matter what you are going through, you are not alone in it.***

Remember this: ***no matter what you are going through, you are not alone in it.***

COUNSEL

1. Refuse to ever think or believe that you are alone in your predicament, God is with you.

For Further Understanding Get This Message: Supernatural Growth And Progress.

BOOK QUOTE ***Depression is the platform to oppression and the pathway to destruction.*** Culled from *22 LAWS OF LIFE* by Dr Paul Enenche

(From Thursday, 4th April, 2013)

38

Victory Over Failure.

'Behold my servant, whom I uphold; mine elect... He shall not fail nor be discouraged, till he have set judgment in the earth: and the isles shall wait for his law' **— ISA 42:1,4**

GOD'S CREATIVE, REDEMPTIVE and prophetic agenda for His people does not include failure. It is not in the nature of God for His children to fail. That does not mean that storms, wind and flood will not arise in life. It only means that no matter what comes against you, you must be on your feet; you must remain standing. To fall is no news; it is refusal to rise that is news.

Micah said, '*Rejoice not against me, O mine enemy when I fall, I shall arise; when I sit in darkness, the LORD shall be light unto me* (Micah 7:8). You may fall but you must not fail. By definition, to fail is to become exhausted, to give out. To fall on the other hand, is to lose balance or drop to the

> **KEY THOUGHT**
>
> ***To fall is no news; it is refusal to rise that is news.***

ground. It means also to decrease or decline. This therefore means that you may lose balance, stagger or even drop to the ground but you must not become exhausted and give out. You must not remain on the ground. Peter staggered, he was sifted as wheat, he denied the Lord, he fell but he did not fail. He rose to become one of the strongest pillars of the early Church. The enemy may cause you to lose balance but you must not crash and remain crashed. The enemy is not excited because you fell; he is excited when you refuse to rise. Understand that failure is not a person; it is not even an event, but an opinion. In other words, you are not a failure because you failed; you are a failure only when you think so!

Remember this: ***to fall is no news; it is refusal to rise that is news***.

COUNSEL

1. Determine not to fail again.
2. Arise from where you failed.
3. Rise up from where you have fallen.

For further understanding get this message: Breaking The Cycle Of Failure Pt. 2

BOOK QUOTE ***When a person behaves as if there is no God, it is a foolish procedure that will definitely end in failure.*** Culled from *21 FOOLISH THINGS PEOPLE DO* by Dr Paul Enenche.

(From Monday, 22nd April, 2013)

39

Don't Give Up!

'If a man die, shall he live again? All the days of my appointed time will I wait, till my change come'
– JOB 14:14

HEREIN LIES THE SECRET of the glorious comeback of Job. He refused to give up, give in or give way to the situation he found himself in. He looked forward to the changes that were ahead. He refused to accept his situation as permanent; he literally refused to die. My counsel is: whenever you have a setback, refuse to take a step back because it is a set-up for a powerful comeback.

When Israel gave in to discouragement in the wilderness by the evil report of the ten spies, (Number 13:32-33), their death sentence was signed. None of them made it to the Promised Land apart from Joshua and Caleb. The rest were already out of existence only waiting to be buried. Please,

refuse to be discouraged with whatever situation you find yourself in. Make the choice to maintain your energy and enthusiasm for survival.

> **KEY THOUGHT**
>
> ***Whenever you have a setback, refuse to take a step back because every setback is a set-up for a powerful comeback.***

The truth is, you will never see anyone achieve anything significant without courage and energy. Emerson said, 'The world belongs to the energetic'. Sir Thomas Buxton said, ' The longer I live, the more deeply I am convinced that what makes the difference between one man and another; the great and the insignificant is energy: that invisible determination, a purpose that once formed, nothing can take away.' With energy, one can do anything that God wants him to do in this world. And no talent, training, opportunity, circumstance will make any headway without it.

Remember this: ***whenever you have a setback, refuse to take a step back because every setback is a set-up for a powerful comeback.***

COUNSEL

1. Never accept any negative situation as a permanent one.
2. Maintain your energy and enthusiasm.

For further understanding get this message: Breaking The Cycle Of Failure Pt. 3

BOOK QUOTE ***When a man has a vision for tomorrow, it gives him strength and wisdom for today.*** Culled from *21 FOOLISH THINGS PEOPLE DO* by Dr Paul Enenche.

(From Sunday, 21st April, 2013)

40

Victory Over Discouragement

'Behold my servant, whom I uphold; mine elect...He shall not fail nor be discouraged, till he have set judgment in the earth in the earth: and the Isles shall wait for his law' – ISA 42:1, 4

EVERY HUMAN BEING CAME to the earth with something to offer and a destiny to fulfil. It takes courage, however, to deliver your relevance and impact to your generation. That is to say, situations that will challenge your courage are going to arise, presenting to you an option to either move ahead in courage or to get established in stagnation by being discouraged.

Discouragement is dissolved or dissipated courage. It is 'diseased' courage. The devil organizes situations around you to steal your courage and lessen your enthusiasm but it must be rejected. The fact is, where courage is lost,

conquest is lost, victory is lost and defeat is established. No conqueror is made without courage.

KEY THOUGHT

No conqueror is made without courage.

What then is courage? I define courage as the energy to survive. It is the enthusiasm to succeed in life. It is a glowing, fiery, aggressive spirit that is ready to fulfil destiny. Courage is the stuff of life; it is the substance of living. Gilbert Chesterton said, 'It is a strong desire to live taking a form of readiness to die.' Courage is not the absence of fear but the movement against fear. It is vitally important to life. To lose this survival energy or enthusiasm is to be like a walking corpse. You do not die when you pass out of your body; you cease to exist meaningfully and gainfully when you lose the courage to exist. Determine to maintain courage.

Remember this: ***no conqueror is made without courage.***

COUNSEL:

1. Never give in to discouragement

For further understanding get this message: Breaking The Cycle Of Failure Part. 2

BOOK QUOTE: ***A cycle of frustration is repeated when lessons are not learnt.*** Culled from *21 FOOLISH THINGS PEOPLE DO* by Dr Paul Enenche.

(From Saturday, 20th April, 2013)

41

Your Joy Determines Your Strength

***Then he said unto them Go your way, eat the fat, and drink the sweet, and send portions unto them whom nothing is prepared: for this day is holy unto our Lord: neither be ye sorry; for the joy of the Lord is your strength.* – NEH. 8:10**

JOY AND PEACE are like a dynamite and a detonator. Your joy determines your strength and your strength determines your victory. And your victory determines your mastery and ability to subdue the earth. It is not possible to subdue anything on earth without joy. Proverb 24:10 says '*if thou faint in the day of adversity, thy strength is small*.'

If joy is equal to strength, and you faint in the midst of battle and adversity, then your joy and by extension, your strength are indeed small. So, the bankruptcy of joy is the scarcity of strength. The shortage of joy is the deficiency

of strength. Anywhere you see joy in short supply, strength will also be in short supply.

Your joy determines your strength, and your strength determines your speed and impact. For instance, if a trailer hits a tree, the impact will be different from when a 'keke NAPEP' (a tricycle) hits a tree. Your weight and strength determines your impact. Do all you can do to defend your joy at all cost.

KEY THOUGHT

The bankruptcy of joy is the scarcity of strength.

Remember this: ***the bankruptcy of joy is the scarcity of strength.***

COUNSEL:

1. Be joyful in every situation.
2. Multiply your strength daily by increasing your praise

For further understanding, get this message: Joy For The Top - Pt 2

BOOK QUOTE: T***o lose your joy is to lose your strength and without strength, there can be no flight.*** Culled from *30 SECRETS TO THE TOP* by Dr Paul Enenche

(Tuesday, 24th September 2013)

42

Shed Every Weight

'Wherefore seeing we also are compassed about with so great a cloud of witnesses, let us lay aside every weight, and the sin which doth so easily beset us, and let us run with patience the race that is set before us'. – HEB. 12:1

AS LONG AS YOU ARE ALIVE, you will face battles. However, as you fight, know that it is only cowards that turn their backs and run from a fight. Convince yourself and make a conscious determination that no situation is too big for you to handle; you are equal to the task. You need to become a possibility-minded person.

Whatever is not in agreement with your vision or what God has told you must be rejected as you proceed on your journey of destiny. Refuse to be distracted and make sure you do not carry extra loads of anxiety, fear, worry, doubt, etc., because they will only slow down your journey. Drop

any weight you are carrying and increase your motion.

KEY THOUGHT

Drop any weight you are carrying and increase your motion.

Also, do not live your life at the mercy of other people's dreams or visions for you. Never entertain or welcome negative people into your life. Gather momentum and make progress. You are responsible for your life under God.

If God says all things are possible and that you can do all things, then join forces with Him. Do not be the one who will call 'impossible' what God has called 'possible' because of the weight you are carrying. Drop it today!

Remember this: ***drop any weight you are carrying and increase your motion.***

COUNSEL

1. Refuse to carry any load of distraction, anxiety, fear, worry, doubt, etc.

For further understanding, get this message: Moving To The Next Level.

BOOK QUOTE ***It is a foolish thing to allow yourself to be enslaved by your fleshly passion… when the rate at which a person masters and conquers his flesh increases, the rate of his progress also increases.*** Culled from *21 FOOLISH THINGS PEOPLE DO* by Dr Paul Enenche.

(From Wednesday, 10th April, 2013)

43

The Battle Of The Mantle

And they said unto him, we have dreamed a dream, and there is no interpreter of it. And Joseph said unto them, Do not interpretations belong to God? Tell me them, I pray you. **GEN 40:8**

EVERY MANTLE WILL ATTRACT a battle, and the area of your mantle will determine the nature of your battle. Joseph, the dreamer and dream interpreter remained in prison for a long time and it appeared as if his dream would not come to pass. Even those whose dreams he had interpreted forgot him in prison (Gen. 40:23). The area where you have answers will be the area where the enemy will confront you with questions. (Abraham, the father of nations, struggled to get the child of promise for about 25years).

What you are meant to pursue will first attempt to pursue you. The area where you have taken a stand is the area the

enemy will try to shake the ground. It is the place where you are anointed that you will be resisted. Never give up your conviction because of your condition or situation. Never give up your mantle because of your battle. The doctor will not give up the practice of medicine because he fell sick. He will prescribe for himself the same medicine he prescribes for other people with similar ailments. The anointing that destroys the yoke in others will destroy your yoke too. Your battle will bow to your mantle. The tap that conducts water will be wet with the water. Re-ignite your conviction by Word-revelation. Your faith will win! If God has put the anointing on you, then that mountain in your life must respect it. Your mantle shall win the battle.

KEY THOUGHT
Never give up your conviction because of your condition or situation.

Remember this: ***never give up your conviction because of your condition or situation.***

COUNSEL

1. Read the text again
2. Meditate deeply on this teaching.

For further understanding, get this message: The Battle Of Destiny.

BOOK QUOTE ***Those who ask for higher 'anointings' are actually asking for higher battle.*** Culled from *THOU ART MY BATTLE AXE* by Dr Paul Enenche.

(From Sunday 10th February, 2013)

44

War Training

'I was also upright before him, and I kept myself from mine iniquity. – Ps. 18:23

AMONG THE THINGS GOD teaches His children are warfare and victory strategies. He is the Lord of Host, the Mighty Man of war. If we are truly the children of our Father, we will be people of war. David said, 'He teacheth my hands to war' (Ps. 18:34).

You do not learn war outside of war. You do not understand victory without conflict. You do not understand deliverance until you are endangered and delivered. Warriors are not made except in the war zone. Hence, when inexplicable conflicts rise up around you, it might not be that you sinned or have a problem or that something is wrong with you; it might be that you are in

a war training, learning war strategies in order to become a warrior and eventually a deliverer.

> **KEY THOUGHT**
>
> ***Out of your misery can come your ministry.***

God allowed the lion and the bear to rise against David and his flock to teach him how to war, turn him into a warrior and a deliverer.

Out of your misery can come your ministry. It is furthermore important to note that the warfare does not come to expose your weakness but to reveal your strength and to show you what God has deposited in you. The conflict is not the focus of the warfare, it is the victory. The conflict came to prove that it is not everybody that can be defeated. You shall come out well!

Remember this: ***out of your misery can come your ministry.***

COUNSEL:

1. Give yourself fully to the training of God.
2. Deploy your training experience against satanic uprisings around you and others.

For further understanding, get this message: What It Takes To Bring Down Giants.

BOOK QUOTE: ***The reason why it bothers you is because you have been packaged to handle it.*** Culled from *GO IN THIS THY MIGHT* by Dr Paul Enenche.

(From Friday 15th February, 2013)

45

Is There Not A Cause?

And David said, what have I now done? Is there not a cause? – 1 SAM. 17:29

THE PURPOSE OF life is a life of purpose. A purpose, at least, should define a person's existence. David's elder brother, Eliab, thought that David was presumptuous when he came out to inquire about what would be done for the man who kills Goliath and David replied with the above question (anchor scripture). Anyone who does not understand his reason for living has no business living. Living without a purpose is like travelling to no destination.

To come into this world and leave it without touching and changing anyone, or making any contribution for human betterment or offering any solution to life is a

tragedy. If your presence is not felt, your absence will not be noticed. The question is, in what way is God glorified and His Kingdom expanded because of you? What vacuum will be created if you are not on earth today?

KEY THOUGHT
Living without a purpose is like travelling to no destination.

Those who live for a purpose do not exist in indifference; they leave their footprints on the sands of time and eternity. They dare any Goliath and provide solutions for their generation. They are not timid but daring. In understanding your purpose, ask your Maker and look within yourself to discover your gifts and talents.

Remember this: ***living without a purpose is like travelling to no destination.***

COUNSEL:

1. Determine to make a difference in your sphere.
2. Fight anything trying to establish you into a life of indifference.

For further understanding, get this message: Living And Fighting For A Cause.

BOOK QUOTE: ***To be purposeful is to be thoughtful. To be thoughtful is to be successful.*** Culled from *30 SECRET TO THE TOP* by Dr Paul Enenche.

(From Saturday 2nd February 2013)

46

The Responsibility Of The Gift.

And so he that had received five talents came and brought other five talents, saying Lord, thou deliveredst unto me five talents: behold I have gained beside them five talent more . – MATT. 25:20

EVERY GIFT, TALENT, GRACE or anointing of God on your life leaves you with a responsibility. The gifts and graces of God are not given for personal pleasure and entertainment. It is not what you have to exhibit in order to feel good.

The Bible said that he that had received the five talents went and traded with the same and gained another five talents.

Your responsibility is the deployment, investment and multiplication of what you have been given. You are meant to put the grace, gift, talent or anointing into very aggressive work until it begins to produce profits, rewards and dividends for the One who gave it to you. It is your responsibility also to multiply the same grace or gifts in the lives of other people on earth. In the study of the scripture, we notice that Joshua did more than Moses; he took Israel into Canaan- which was what Moses could not achieve.

It is also recorded that Elisha did more Miracles than Elijah. Theologians said that while Elijah performed sixteen miracles, Elisha performed thirty-two miracles, the last one being in his grave when a dead man was raised after coming in contact with his bones. When, however, successful and outstanding prophets of Old Testament were to be recognised in the New Testament (At the mountain of transfiguration), it was Moses and Elijah and not Joshua and Elisha. One reason for that, I think is that Joshua and Elisha multiplied the grace on their lives into nobody whereas Moses and Elijah took their time to pour themselves into them. Success is incomplete without the deployment, investment, and multiplication of the grace into others. Accept responsibility! Develop and deploy the grace of God on your life to your generation.

KEY THOUGHT

Success is incomplete without the deployment, investment and multiplication of the grace.

Remember this: ***success is incomplete without the deployment, investment and multiplication of the grace. God bless you!***

COUNSEL:

1. Become a people developer. Multiply the grace of God on your life into others: subordinate, spouse etc.
2. Also, profit the Kingdom by putting your gifts into work to make the lives of other people in your generation better.

For further understanding, get this message: Blessed Above All.

BOOK QUOTE ***Anybody who does not value and invest in people will have a frustrated future.*** Culled from *365 WISDOM CAPSULES* by Dr Paul Enenche.

(From Tuesday, 21 August, 2012)

47

The Risk Of Investment.

***He which received the one talent came and said, Lord, I know thee that thou art an hard man, reaping where thou has not sown, and gathering where thou hast not strewed: And I was afraid, and went and hid the talent in the earth; lo, there thou has that is thine.* – MATTHEW 25:24-25.**

IN LIFE, THERE IS NO INVESTMENT without risk; you don't have a chance if you don't take a chance. You can't succeed if you can't attempt. If you can't risk failing, you can't help failing. Those who are afraid of failure definitely fail. Among other things, the problem with the man in our anchor text was the fear of taking risks. He did not want to lose the talent in investment so he decided to save it. He eventually lost everything. In order not to end a loser in life, you must make up your mind to become a risk taker. Impact makers are risk takers. Great impact is the product of great risk-sponsored effort.

It was William Carey who once said, '*Attempt great things for*

God, achieve great things for God!' That is, in order to achieve great things for God, you must attempt great things for God. God Almighty Himself is actually a great risk-taker. When He sent and invested His Son Jesus Christ for the sake of the redemption of mankind, it was a great risk. How would people believe that He really died for them? How about suffering so tremendously and nobody believes? It was a great risk but it is producing great results. To multiply and maximise the grace, gifts, talents and resources of your life, you must decide to be a risk-taker. Be more focused on your desired results than on any possible loss. Determine to rise up again and again even if repeated attempts fail. Be willing to be laughed at or scorned if possible until you reach your goal. There can be no rise without risk and no reach without stretch.

KEY THOUGHT

Great impact is the product of great risk-sponsored effort.

Remember this: ***great impact is the product of great risk-sponsored effort.***

COUNSEL

1. Ensure the risk you take is in line with the will of God for your life.
2. Do as the key thought implies

For further understanding, get this message: The Measure Of Life.

BOOK QUOTE ***There is no rise without risk. And there is no reach without risk.*** Culled from *30 SECRETS TO THE TOP* by Dr Paul Enenche.

(From Thursday 23th August 2012)

48

Oil Cannot Be Borrowed

And the foolish said unto the wise, give us of your oil; for our lamps are gone out. But the wise answered…not so; lest there be not enough for us and you: but go ye rather to them that sell, and buy for yourselves. **– MATTHEW25:8-9**

THE PATHETIC STORY in the Bible passage above shows that everyone needs to be in possession of the oil (anointing of the Lord) all the time. The reason is that, you do not know the emergencies that will arise around you requiring the engagement of the anointing of the Lord.

The truth is, the time will come in life when the anointing on somebody else will not answer to the challenges of your life. You have to apply the anointing on your own life to handle that challenge at that time. And if you don't have any anointing on your life at such a time, you could end in defeat and become a victim of unpreparedness in life's battle. I pray that that will not be your portion in Jesus' Name.

The other very important issue here is that the oil (the anointing) cannot be borrowed. It has to be purchased. What does that mean? It means that you have to pay a price; you give something in exchange for the precious anointing of God. The first price is the release of your time in fellowshipping with God: worshipping your

> **KEY THOUGHT**
>
> ***If you need the oil, you must pay the price.***

Maker, studying His Words, fasting and praying. The second price is the surrender of pride, ostentation and self-centeredness. You must give them up if you need the precious oil. The third is the elimination of iniquity, uncleanness, impurity, unrighteousness; you must give them up if you need the precious oil; the anointing. The fourth price is attention and submission to spiritual authority for impartation. There are many more things which the Spirit will reveal to those who really desire the oil. If you need the oil, you must pay the price.

Remember this: ***if you need the oil, you must pay the price.***

COUNSEL

1. Start paying your price for the oil now.
2. What dimension of the anointing do you desire? Search the Scripture for the relevant price and ask the Holy Spirit to reveal other things you need to know to you.

For further understanding, get this messages: Wisdom Keys For Survival

BOOK QUOTE ***Those who slumber the slumber of prayerlessness and slothfulness never experience God. God's programme is always revealed to the diligent.*** Culled from *REASON FOR LIVING* by Dr Paul Enenche.

(From Saturday 18th August, 2012)

49

The Spirit Is Willing

Watch and pray, that ye enter not into temptation! The spirit indeed is willing, but the flesh is weak.
– Matthew 26:41

YOU WILL NEVER GET anything done if you allow your flesh to rule your life. It was by surrendering his life to the desires of the flesh that Esau sold his birth right and lost his destiny. Understand that most of the time, what your flesh wants is contrary to both your spiritual life and destiny. To follow the flesh is to end up as a failure. The flesh must merely be the vehicle for your life and the spirit (the real you) must be the driver. When a driver loses control of the vehicle, disaster is inevitable.

In the same manner, if you are unable to maintain a firm grip on your flesh, both spiritual and destiny disasters are inevitable. The spirit indeed is willing, but the flesh is weak. It is crucial to know that willingness is good but it is not enough to get you to your high places in God. It has

been said that, 'if wishes were horses, even beggars would have ridden on them.' The Bible did not say, 'if you are willing and **complacent**, you will eat the good of the land' but 'if you are willing and **obedient**, you will eat the good of the land' (Isaiah 1:19). The willingness of the spirit must therefore translate into the obedience of the flesh for a solid spiritual life to be developed. Do all you can to ensure that your flesh obeys the 'promptings' of your spirit. Watch and pray that you enter not into temptation! Let your spirit take the lead and let the flesh follow.

KEY THOUGHT

To follow the flesh is to end up as a failure.

Remember this: ***to follow the flesh is to end a failure. God bless you!***

COUNSEL:

1. At the place of prayer, handle the spirit of apathy and prayerlessness.
2. Continually apply for the grace to exercise mastery over the flesh.

For further understanding, get this message: 'The Product Of Death To Flesh.

BOOK QUOTE: To conquer anything in this world, you must first conquer yourself. Culled from *21 FOOLISH THINGS PEOPLE DO* by Dr Paul Enenche.

(From Saturday 4th August, 2012)

50

You Can Do All Things

I can do all things through Christ which strengtheneth me. **– PHILIPPIANS 4:13**

GOD HAS INVESTED so much in you that He expects you to be able to do all things, provided they line up with His will. That is why the Scripture says, '*all things are possible to him that believeth*' (Mark 9:23). If you say you can you are right. And if you say you can't, you are also right. All things are possible to all who believe they are.

It does not matter how long the situation has persisted, if you can only believe, things will turn around for good. Like the invalid in John 5:1-9 who for thirty-eight (38) years could not be helped until the moment he agreed with Jesus that he could be healed, your moment of change will come when you agree with God that you can do all things.

As long as you say, 'I have HIV, arthritis, cancer, etc., the

KEY THOUGHT

Your moment of change will come when you agree with God.

situation will remain like that. But to see the end of those conditions, you have to see the situation as non-existent. Our Father, God, is the One who '*Calleth those things that be not as though they were*' Romans 4:17. Do you believe you have the form and likeness of your Father (God)? Then, do likewise. For everyone who is connected to Christ, the Anointed One, there is a continuous supply of anointing, ability or energy that makes you equal to every emergency. That is, the ability to surmount every obstacle is permanently available. There is a grace to tackle every challenge through Christ and His anointing! It doesn't matter the task facing you, you are equal to it, in Jesus' Name!

Remember this: ***your moment of change will come when you agree with God.***

COUNSEL:

1. Erase the word **'IMPOSSIBILITY'** from your mentality today
2. At every junction of life, walk in the reality of Philippians 4:13

For further understanding, get this message: Armed For The Journey.

BOOK QUOTE: ***Any time you have the vision and conviction, and you step out in action, God will supply the unction for the manifestation of your expectations.*** Culled from *365 WISDOM CAPSULES* by Dr Paul Enenche.

(From Friday 10th September, 2010)

51

The Nature Of Spiritual Warfare.

For though we walk in the flesh, we do not war after the flesh: For the weapons of our warfare are not carnal, but mighty through God to the pulling down of strongholds; casting down imaginations, and every high thing that exalteth itself against the knowledge of God, and bringing into captivity every thought to the obedience of Christ." -2 Cor. 10:3-5

WHAT COMES TO YOUR MIND when you read this portion of scripture? A call to warfare, isn't it? The fact however, is, the battle of life is not only the one fought in the physical but in the mind also. The battle in the physical is a fall-out of the one in the mind.

The four things we are contending with are:

1. Strongholds
2. Imaginations
3. High things that exalt themselves against the knowledge of God.
4. Thoughts

When it comes to the matter of distracting a man from his purpose, the devil is a master-strategist. He knows how to invade the mind with the above mentioned things. Your responsibility, therefore, is to develop your mind to be able to resist and overcome satan and the thoughts he floods your mind with. A weak mind means a weak destiny.

> **KEY THOUGHT**
>
> ***A weak mind means a weak destiny.***

Since satan will never stop trying to distract and dissuade you, you must also never stop ensuring that your mind is constantly being developed against him. What is the secret of developing your mind? The Word of God. Study it as if your life depends on it because in reality, it does. When the mind is filled, both with the Word of God and anointed materials, negative thoughts may come but they go immediately because there is no vacuum for them in the mind.

Remember this: ***a weak mind means a weak destiny.***

COUNSEL:

1. Become a Word addict by strictly following the daily Bible reading plan.
2. Reply every negative thought with a Scripture, backed possibly by positive declarations

For further understanding, get this message: Too Anointed And Protected To Be Arrested.

BOOK QUOTE: ***It is what crosses your mind that crosses your life.*** Culled from *365 WISDOM CAPSULES* by Dr Paul Enenche.

(From Saturday 18th September, 2010)

52

From Rejection To Distinction

***And the Lord said unto Samuel, how long wilt thou mourn for Saul, seeing that I have rejected him from reigning over Israel? Fill thine horn with oil, and go, and I will send thee to Jesse the Bethlehemite: For I have provided me a king among his sons.* – 1 SAMUEL 16:1**

THE ANOINTING was not what made David king. God had confirmed his kingship before the anointing. That was why God said, '... I have provided me a king among his sons.' All that was required to make him king was already in him. No one could deny him the throne. It was his God-ordained destiny. The anointing came to authenticate, validate, consolidate and manifest his royal destiny.

Interestingly however, David was ignored by his own father at that crucial moment. He was rejected and relegated yet, all that didn't rule out the fact that he was the

king. Don't allow your challenges to depress your soul because they actually do not rule out the fact that you are who God says you are.

> **KEY THOUGHT**
>
> ***Your rejection positions you for your distinction.***

I have discovered that your rejection positions you for your distinction. Where you are resisted the most is where you will be anointed the most. Your opposition is the platform for your promotion. Those who look at you and conclude that you will never amount to anything in life are about to be disappointed. God is a specialist at turning nothing into something. If everybody is against you and God is on your side, then you are a winner. I heartily congratulate you if you are currently experiencing opposition. That opposition will lead you to your position in life. You are not what men say you are. You are what God says you are.

Remember this: ***your rejection positions you for your distinction***

COUNSEL:

1. Celebrate yourself and what God is about to manifest through your life.
2. Move around with a good air of dignity.

For further understanding, get this message: Restoring Your Originality.

BOOK QUOTE: ***At times, the devil thinks he is resisting you without knowing that he is assisting you.*** Culled from *365 WISDOM CAPSULES* by Dr Paul Enenche.

(From Thursday 23th September, 2010)

53

Make The Most Of Your Time

Redeeming the time, because the days are evil
– EPHESIANS 5:16

AMONG THE PRECIOUS GIFTS of God to mankind is time. Time is given to help man to achieve purpose and destiny. Time is a servant that is calculated to make men outstanding masters of life. Also, time is a servant meant to be directed, employed, engaged or assigned. Wastage of life and destiny is the outcome when time is unemployed. Life is a burden; existence is a misery when time is not directed. The counsel from our anchor Scripture is: make the very most of time, buying up each opportunity because the days are evil.

Maximally utilise your time; don't lose time. Don't permit time to pass without progress being made. To complain

> **KEY THOUGHT**
> ***Time is a servant that is calculated to make outstanding masters of life.***

that there is no time means that a lot of time wastage is going on. There is time to do anything you want to do in life if you really mean business. All you need to do is to allocate time to purpose or agenda. Determine what must be done and determine when (day, week, month or year) it must be done. You don't really want to do anything until you have determined when to do it. Those who make the most of time make their mark in life. They achieve more in one month than some achieve in an entire lifetime. They achieve more in one lifetime than most achieve in one hundred lifetimes put together. William Carey was one of such men. As a Missionary to India, he translated the Bible into forty-three Indian dialects within eight years. Endeavour to make the most of your time!

Remember this: ***time is a servant that is calculated to make men outstanding masters of life.***

COUNSEL

1. Go ahead; do as the lesson teaches- allocate time to every activity.
2. Trust God not to waste time.

For further understanding, get this message: Secret Of Fulfilment.

BOOK QUOTE *To live a quality life, you must fill your time with quality activities.* Culled from *365 WISDOM CAPSULES* by Dr Paul Enenche.

(From Sunday 10th June, 2012)

54

Beware Of Pride

But he giveth more grace. Wherefore he saith, God resisteth the proud, but giveth grace unto the humble.
– JAMES 4:6

PRIDE IS THE MOST dangerous and destructive character trait anyone can possess. It is a major factor in the abortion of destiny. Lucifer, a.k.a satan the devil lost his dignity and authority to pride. He wanted to be like the Most High (Isa. 14:12-15). Adam and Eve lost their place in the garden because they fell to the same prideful temptation to 'eat the forbidden fruit and be like God' (Gen 3:5). Pride was the first sin ever to be committed. It is the nature of Lucifer. It brings back to God's memory the initial rebellion of the devil.

Pride makes you feel bigger than you really are. It gives you an exaggerated opinion or inflated idea of yourself. It is the sponsor of arrogance. It makes you look down and

talk down on people. It makes you give yourself credit for what God is doing in your (own or others) life. It gives you an ar ival m ntality. It makes you immune to counsel, advic or instruction.

> **KEY THOUGHT**
>
> ***God assists everyone but He resists the proud.***

It is the foundation for destruction. God assists everyone but He resists the proud. If the devil resists you, you can be assisted. But if God resists you, who can rescue you? To be full of pride is to be empty of grace. Grace is only available to the humble. And to lack grace is to fall flat since we stand by grace (Romans 11:20). Many sudden fall into sin is rooted in pride among other things.

Never forget that without Him, you can do nothing.

Remember this: ***God assists everyone but He resist the proud.***

COUNSEL

1. Always remain little in your own eyes.
2. Never forget where God took you from.

For further understanding, get this message: Secret Of Fulfilment.

BOOK QUOTE ***When you think your wealth is your making… or the anointing you carry is your making, God will withdraw from you a little, so you can see how naked you are without Him. Culled from*** *THOU ART MY BATTLE AXE* by Dr Paul Enenche.

(From 25th February, 2013)

55

Daily Fire

***And the fire upon the alter shall be burning in it; it shall not be put out: and the priest shall burn wood on it every morning, and lay the burnt offering in order upon it; and he shall burn thereon the fat of the peace offerings.* – LEV. 6:12**

THE MAINTENANCE of a consistently constant spiritual temperature is critical to a productive spiritual life.

Never let your spiritual fire go out! Never lack zeal or reduce in energy and passion. In fact, the ideal situation is to be progressively increasing in spiritual intensity. God has no stationary positions for His children because '*the path of the just is as a bright shining light, that shineth more and more unto the perfect day*' (Prov. 4:18). The man of God, Smith Wigglesworth, who was used powerfully of God to raise twenty-three (23) dead people said 'It is a tragedy to remain on the same spiritual plane for two consecutive

days.' If you have stopped going forward, you have started going backward. Backsliding is not only backward motion into sin but absence of forward motion into God. The secret of constant fire is appearing before God daily in devotion and worship. There is fresh fire, fresh bread, fresh manna for each day. The reason is that yesterday's fire cannot handle today's cold; yesterday's bread cannot quench today's hunger, yesterday's mantle cannot handle today's battle. Every new day requires new grace. Go before God daily and early to rekindle your fire.

KEY THOUGHT

Backsliding is not only backward motion into sin, but absence of forward motion into God.

Remember this: ***backsliding is not only backward motion into sin, but absence of forward motion into God.***

COUNSEL

1. Assess your current spiritual temperature.
2. Rekindle the fire of passion for His Presence.

For further understanding, get this message: Acquire The Fire.

BOOK QUOTE ***When fire is lacking, prayerlessness is established.*** Culled from *365 WISDOM CAPSULES* by Dr Paul Enenche.

(From Tuesday 26th February, 2013)

56

In Everything Give Thanks

***In everything give thanks: for this is the will of God in Christ Jesus concerning you.* – 1 THESS. 5:18**

IN EVERY SITUATION we find ourselves, there is something to thank God for. If you have a problem, God is the reason why it is not worse than it is now. I was angry because I did not wake up one morning as early as I should. Before the devil could use it against me, I realised that my own challenge was that I did not wake up on time to pray whereas there were those who did not wake up at all that day. They slept and died. I also realised that whereas I was angry that I overslept, there are those who can pay any amount in order to have a good sweet sleep at night. The situation may be bad but it is never totally bad. God's servant, Pastor E. A. Adeboye told a story of a man who was dancing and jubilating on the highway after

armed robbers snatched his car. When asked the reason behind his action, he said:

1. I thank God that it was my car they took and not my life.
2. I thank God that I have something good enough for someone to steal.
3. I thank God that I am not the one who stole; I am the one they stole from.

KEY THOUGHT

The situation may be bad, but it is never totally bad.

What a mentality! Many times, the enemy keeps our eyes on the problem so we cannot see God's goodness. If only you can learn to give thanks in everything, i.e., to see reasons for thanking God in everything, then you will frustrate the agenda of the devil and provoke God's counsel on your life.

Remember this: ***the situation may be bad, but it is never totally bad.***

COUNSEL

1. Spend time today to thank God for your life.
2. Make it a habit to thank Him always.

For further understanding, get this message: The Power Of Thanks

KEY QUOTE: ***Everybody praise God under certain conditions but real worshipers praise God under all conditions.*** Culled from *365 WISDOM CAPSULES* by Dr Paul Enenche.

(From Saturday 23rd February, 2013)

57 The Reason For Delayed Divine Intervention

***And in the fourth watch of the night Jesus went unto them, walking on the sea.* – MATT. 14:25**

WHENEVER GOD DELAYS in showing up in our lives in a persistent, challenging situation despite persistent prayers, we are often discouraged. However, God delays sometimes because He is preparing something better and greater for us. In today's anchor Scripture, Jesus sent His disciples to cross over to the other side in the evening (that is in the first watch), but He did not surface to rescue them from the raging storm that confronted them until the fourth watch. (The first watch is between 6-9 pm while the fourth watch is between 3-6am.) A journey that should have taken 30 minutes by ship took almost 13 hours. Why did the Master delay like this? When the Master delays, it is to confirm the enemy's defeat. When the devil has done his worst, then the stage is set for God to do His best. If God's intervention seems to be delayed in your life, it is because He wants to confirm the 'yeyeciousness' (hopelessness) of the devil and manifest His 'agidigbaciouness' (Almightiness). He delays to show the challenge that some people cannot be defeated.

He appeared to Shadrach, Meshach, and Abednego when they were already in the fire to show the world that the fire could not burn them. He didn't come when they were arrested or tied up but when they were put into the fire to show them that He could defeat any challenge. The devil is eternally a loser. In a similar vein, Jesus did not appear the first day Lazarus died but on the fourth day, when Lazarus was already stinking in order to reveal to the kingdom of darkness that despite the delay, no challenge is too big for God to handle. Delay is not a barrier to God. Whenever God seems to delay in showing up in an issue, it is because He wants to come out in a big and mighty way. Get set because something big is coming your way.

KEY THOUGHT
When the devil has done his worst, then the stage is set for God to do His best.

Remember this: ***when the devil has done his worst, then the stage is set for God to do His best.***

COUNSEL

1. Make up your mind not to give up in the midst of what looks like a delayed Divine intervention.
2. Look out for what God has promised you and give Him the praise.

For further understanding, get this message: Riding The Storm Of Life.

BOOK QUOTE ***When it is coming late, it is coming heavy*** Culled from *365 WISDOM CAPSULE* by Dr Paul Enenche.

(From Tuesday 5th May, 2009)

58

You Are Almost There

***But when he saw the wind boisterous, he was afraid; and beginning to sink, he cried, saying, Lord, save me. And immediately Jesus stretched forth his hand, and caught him, and said unto him, o thou of little faith, wherefore didst thou doubt?* – MATT. 14:30-31**

IF YOU WANT TO SUCCEED in life, you must walk by faith; you must depend on the instruction of God. This was how Peter was able to walk on water. But when the wind arose, he became afraid and began to sink. From today's anchor Scripture, we can see that Peter had almost reached where Jesus was before he became afraid and began to sink. He was just a stone's throw away from Jesus; he was almost there.

Many people give up on God when they are almost at the verge of their breakthrough. Peter was just a stone's throw away from the Master; he would have completed his journey had he taken a few more steps. But he allowed his sight to drown his faith and fear set in. Next thing was he began to sink. Beloved, fear is a sinker of life and destiny. He looked at the storm, became afraid and began to sink. Please never take your eyes off your Master.

Many young ladies have endured and kept themselves pure for a long time but decided to compromise when they felt that they had waited too long for a husband.

They compromised at the verge of God's breakthrough for their lives. Many people give up at the brink of victory. Fear usually comes in at the point where you are about to succeed. Many people want to change their minds and go against God's will when God is about to give them a breakthrough. The truth is, the journey backward is longer than the journey forward. The Master is closer to you than the storm; you will not sink. Jesus is nearer than the danger. Don't lose consciousness of His presence and allow the storm to sink you; the solution is closer than the danger.

KEY THOUGHT
Many people give up on God when they are almost at the verge of their breakthrough.

The Bible says, 'they that endure till the end shall be saved' (Matt. 24:13). It is too late to compromise now; you are almost there. God is about to change your situation; don't give up.

COUNSEL:

1. Make a determination not to give up on God despite the terrible challenge you might be passing through.
2. Hold on to God's Word to the end.

For further understanding get this message: Riding The Storm Of Life

BOOK QUOTE: ***Those who wait on the Lord cannot waste in life. Those who trust in God cannot rust in life.*** Culled from *30 SECRETS TO THE TOP* by Dr Paul Enenche.

(From Mon. Sept. 9th, 2003)

59

Keys To His Presence

And the third day there was a marriage in Cana of Galilee; and the mother of Jesus was there: And both Jesus was called, and his disciples, to the marriage. **– JOHN 2:1-2**

GOD IS PRESENT where He is valued, respected and celebrated. He is present where He is needed. Jesus was not invited to the wedding at Cana of Galilee to perform a miracle, but because He was valued so much that they believed that the occasion could not hold without Him. God is present where He is pursued. There are so many miracle seekers, and very few God seekers in the Church today. The question is, what do you value the most in your life? Many of us are very particular about what we wear, our hairstyles, cars, etc. I wish we could place such level of value for God in our lives.

How do you communicate your value for something? By the price you are ready to offer for it of course. The price you are willing to pay for something is what communicates the value you have for that thing. When a man loves and wants to marry a woman, he is ready to pay the bride-price and fulfil the necessary conditions in order to marry her. Some men will say they want to marry some ladies but keep them waiting for 3-5 years and even much more in certain cases. They say they like them so much yet they keep them waiting. It is price that communicates value. What price are you willing to pay in your relationship with God? In your pursuit of God, how much of your time are you willing and ready to spend with Him? How much of your resources will you invest in His cause? It determines how much of His presence you will carry. The reason why we don't manifest the same level of the Presence of God is because we don't pay the same price. We do not have the same dimension of God's Presence because we don't have the same sense of value for Him.

KEY THOUGHT

The price you are willing to pay for something is what communicates the value you have for that thing.

Remember this: ***the price you are willing to pay for something is what communicates the value you have for that thing.***

COUNSEL:

1. Endeavour to surround your environment with His worship and praise.
2. Show God how much you value Him by having quality communion time with Him

For further understanding, get this message: The Power Of His Presence - Pt 3 The Power Of His Presence - Pt 3

BOOK QUOTE: ***The quality of your offering to God determines the value you place on Him.*** Culled from *365 WISDOM CAPSULES* by Dr Paul Enenche.

(From Sunday, 12th October 2014)

60

Spirit Of Violence

And from the days of John the Baptist until now the kingdom of heaven suffereth violence, and the violent take it by force. **– MATT. 11:12**

SPIRITUAL VIOLENCE is very critical to total victory in life. Now, why do you need violence? You need violence because there are demons and witches who try to stop the arrival of what is yours. God told the Israelites in Deuteronomy 2:24, 'I have given into thine hand Sihon the Amorite, king of Heshbon, and his land: begin to possess it, and contend with him in battle.' That means, the Israelites could not possess their possession without contending with the enemy; and that requires the spirit of violence. The spirit of violence refers to that aggressive spirit of a fighter; refusal to give in to defeat or to make the devil feel like he is a winner. It is remaining in the fight until your healing, fruit of the womb, miracle or anointing arrives. Unfortunately, some of us quit too easily.

I know of a man who trusted God for the healing of his heart for 21 years and his healing came. I heard of a woman with arthritis who sang in the choir in Kathrine Khulman's ministry. She kept singing, and all the while, other people were getting healed but she was not, healed for 13 solid years. Eventually her healing came after years of persistence and consistency. And your own is coming right now. Maybe you have been waiting for a long time, but now is the time for your healing. Your degree of violence determines your degree of victory. And violence is not a function of gender because some women can be more violent than some men. Every time you are tolerant, the devil becomes unusually aggressive. Let the devil see your eyes and know that you are no longer patient. '*Resist the devil, and he will flee from you*'. James 4:7

KEY THOUGHT

Your degree of violence determines your degree of victory.

Remember this: ***your degree of violence determines your degree of victory.***

COUNSEL

1. Get the recommended message and listen to it.
2. Make up your mind to wear out the devil and not the other way round.

For further understanding, get this message: Acquire The Fire.

BOOK QUOTE ***If you have made up your mind to get to the top, then you have made up your mind to be a fighter.*** Culled from *30 SECRETS TO THE TOP* by Dr Paul Enenche.

(From Tuesday, 14th October 2014)